BEYOND MOUNT SI

THE BEST HIKES WITHIN
85 MILES OF SEATTLE

BEYOND MOUNT SI

THE BEST HIKES WITHIN 85 MILES OF SEATTLE

by John Zilly

ADVENTURE PRESS
SEATTLE, WASHINGTON

Copyeditor: Erin Moore
Cover and interior design: Peter D'Agostino
Cover photo: Cliff Leight
Interior photographs: John Zilly, Spencer Harris, Wade Praeger
Maps: John Zilly
Proofreader: Emily Bedard
Research assistance: Spencer Harris

ISBN: 1-881583-08-2

Adventure Press
P.O. Box 14059, Seattle, Washington 98114
206-200-2578, 206-568-0592 (f)
adventurepress.com

Adventure Press books are always printed in the U.S. on recycled paper.

Disclaimer: Have fun out there, but be safe and use common sense. The author and publisher of *Beyond Mount Si* disclaim and are in no way responsible or liable for the consequences of using this guide. Hiking can be dangerous. The difficulty of the trails described in this guide and the level of experience required to safely hike on these trails are subjective. It is incumbent on each person to assess his or her preparedness for a trail in light of his or her own skills, experience, and equipment. The information contained in this book, as of the date of publication, is as accurate as possible. But conditions on these routes can and do change quickly.

To my parents, for teaching me about trails.

And to Dova and Sam,
For being wonderful hiking companions, present and future.

Many thanks to Spencer Harris. This book couldn't have been completed without your help. Thanks also to Marea Angela Castañeda for your love and patience, Jim Emery for your ideas and the inspiration, Peter D'Agostino for the great design, David Graves for just about everything, Kate Rogers for guidance, and Craig Bartlett, Wade Praeger, Mark Reudink, and Greg Strong for slogging it out on those longest days.

OVERVIEW MAP

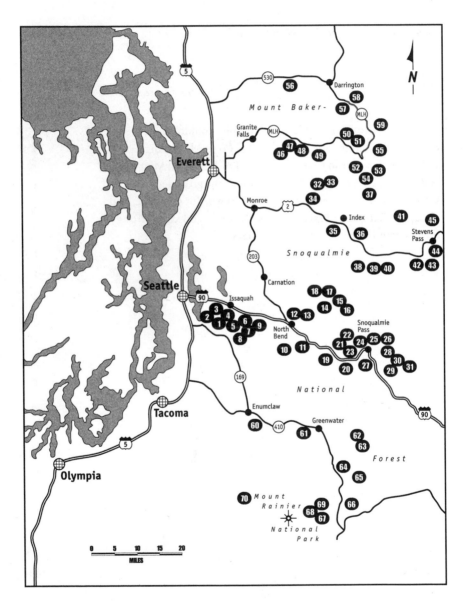

CONTENTS

CONTENTS

HIKES BY DIFFICULTY

EASY

Hike#	Hike Name	Best Season	Kids	Fee
3	Anti-Aircraft Peak	spring summer fall winter	kids!	
27	Snoqualmie Tunnel	spring summer fall	kids!	yes
36	Barclay Lake	summer fall	kids!	yes
60	Mud Mountain Rim	spring summer fall winter	kids!	
62	Greenwater Lakes	spring summer fall	kids!	yes

INTERMEDIATE

Hike#	Hike Name	Best Season	Kids	Fee
2	De Leo Wall	spring summer fall winter		
5	Squak Mountain	spring summer fall winter	kids!	yes
8	Talus Rocks	spring summer fall winter	kids!	
11	Twin Falls	spring summer fall winter	kids!	yes
21	Talapus Lake	summer fall	kids!	yes
38	Lake Dorothy	summer fall	kids!	yes
61	Federation Forest	spring summer fall	kids!	yes
70	Green Lake	summer fall	kids!	yes

DIFFICULT

Hike#	Hike Name	Best Season	Kids	Fee
1	Wilderness Peak	spring summer fall winter	kids!	
4	Bear Ridge	spring summer fall winter	kids!	
7	West Tiger Mtn 3	spring summer fall winter		
9	Dwight's Way	spring summer fall winter		
12	Little Mount Si	spring summer fall winter	kids!	
13	Mount Si	spring summer fall		
14	Middle Fork of the Snoqualmie River	spring summer fall	kids!	yes

HIKES BY DIFFICULTY

DIFFICULT ⛰ ⛰ ⛰

Hike#	Hike Name	Best Season	Kids	Fee
20	Annette Lake	summer fall	kids!	yes
24	Melakwa Lake	summer fall		yes
25	Snow Lake	summer fall		yes
29	Margaret Lake	summer fall	kids!	yes
32	Boulder Lake	summer fall		
33	Big Greider Lake	summer fall		
34	Wallace Falls	spring summer fall	kids!	yes
35	Lake Serene	summer fall	kids!	yes
42	Surprise Creek	summer fall		yes
44	Josephine Lake	summer fall		yes
46	Mount Pilchuck	summer fall		yes
47	Heather Lake	summer fall	kids!	yes
48	Lake Twentytwo	summer fall	kids!	yes
49	Cutthroat Lakes	summer fall		
55	Goat Lake	summer fall		yes
56	Boulder River	spring summer fall	kids!	yes
57	Peek-a-boo Lake	summer fall		yes
58	White Chuck Bench	spring summer fall	kids!	yes
63	Lost Lake	summer fall		yes
64	Snoquera Falls	summer fall		yes
65	Noble Knob	summer fall	kids!	yes
66	Crystal Lakes	summer fall		
67	Summer Land	summer fall	kids!	yes
68	Glacier Basin–Mount Rainier	summer fall		yes
69	Upper Palisades Lake	summer fall		yes

HIKES BY DIFFICULTY

MOST DIFFICULT ⛰ ⛰ ⛰ ⛰

Hike#	Hike Name	Best Season	Kids	Fee
6	West Tiger Rambler	spring summer fall winter		
10	Rattlesnake Mtn	spring summer fall		
15	Hester Lake	summer fall		yes
16	Myrtle Lake	summer fall		yes
18	Snoqualmie Lake	summer fall		yes
19	McClellan Butte	summer fall		yes
22	Pratt Lake	summer fall		yes
23	Granite Mountain	summer fall		yes
26	Kendall Katwalk	summer fall		yes
28	Alaska Lake	summer fall		
30	Lake Lillian	summer fall		yes
31	Rampart Lakes	summer fall		yes
37	Blanca Lake	summer fall		yes
39	Big Heart Lake	summer fall ·		yes
40	Necklace Valley	summer fall		yes
41	Pear Lake	summer fall		yes
43	Thunder Mountain	summer fall		yes
45	Lake Valhalla	summer fall		yes
50	Mount Forgotten Mdws	summer fall		yes
51	Dickerman Mountain	summer fall		yes
52	Gothic Basin	summer fall		yes
53	Glacier Basin–Monte Cristo	summer fall		yes

EPIC ⛰ ⛰ ⛰ ⛰ ⛰

Hike#	Hike Name	Best Season	Kids	Fee
17	Nordrum Lake	summer fall		yes
54	Twin Lakes	summer fall		yes
59	Mount Pugh	summer fall		yes

BEYOND MOUNT SI

The South and Middle Forks of the Snoqualmie River meet near North Bend, and it's here the steep slopes of Mount Si shoot straight up from the valley floor. From a distance, its location at the edge of the valley gives Mount Si an air of imposing drama, even if it just barely peeks over the 4,000-foot mark. The drama doesn't subside on the trail, either—it's a steep, challenging hike, with a rocky top that affords long views.

Our backyard hike, Mount Si made many of us hikers. But nowadays it's become one of the most crowded hikes around. And in our daily rush and buzz, it's easy to forget that the Cascades and foothills near Seattle are full of beautiful trails for day hiking and backpacking. That's why this book exists. You don't necessarily have to climb higher or drive farther to find great hikes. You'll find all the best hikes close to Seattle right here, in the next 200 pages of *Beyond Mount Si*. These 70 hikes, from 3 to 18 miles, range from pleasant walks along rivers and enchanting forest paths to challenging hikes up high peaks to hidden mountain lakes. Whatever your favorite terrain, it's time to get out onto the trails and discover beautiful adventures.

CHOOSING A HIKE

What do you want in a hike? How about a beautiful trail that matches your hiking temperament, be it opossum or mountain goat. And of course you don't want to have any trouble reaching the trailhead or finding your way along the route. Welcome to *Beyond Mount Si*. You won't find a guidebook that makes it easier to select a great trail or to follow the route, whether it's getting to the trailhead in the first place or getting *back* to the trailhead at the end of the day. Okay, I can get a little obsessive, and parts of the trail descriptions can get to sounding complicated; don't worry, you'll appreciate the precise detail (and it'll make sense) when confronted with a not-so-intuitive 5-way intersection. It's my job to get lost, not yours.

Of course this guidebook has lots of nifty features besides directions, like GPS coordinates, elevation profiles, phone numbers, Web addresses, and a gazetteer for each hike that lists nearby camping and services. The following section describes the book's rating system, explains how the information is presented, and provides an annotated look at some of the wording conventions I use to describe each hike.

Difficulty Rating

The difficulty rating for each hike is measured in peaks, ranging from one to five, with one peak being easiest and five peaks designating long haul epics. You'll find this quick reference at the top of each hike. The difficulty rating is based on the length of the hike, the steepness of the hills, the cumulative elevation gain, and the condition of the trail. Remember there can be a range of difficulty within each rating, especially among the three-peak hikes. Always read through the Trail Notes and The Hike description to evaluate your selection.

EASY: Just about everyone should be able to make it through a one-peak hike. These trails range from 3 to 6 miles, usually have cumulative elevation gains of less than 800 feet, and should generally be smooth, comfortable walking. Many of these are perfect for families.

INTERMEDIATE: Two-peak hikes can be as long as 8 miles, but generally have less than 1,000 feet of cumulative elevation gain. You'll probably find some steep sections, but the trail should be mostly smooth.

DIFFICULT: Many hikes receive the three-peak rating. These trails are between 4 and 13 miles, with cumulative elevation gains from 1,000 to 2,200 feet. They are either longer, well-maintained trails with smaller elevation gains or shorter and steeper trails that require more hiking agility. Note that although these routes are rated half way between easy and extreme, they are defined as difficult because, well, climbing over 1,000 feet is a workout.

MOST DIFFICULT: These hikes range from 6 to 16 miles in length and may have elevation gains up to 4,500 feet. Every one of these routes comes with some steep, relentless climbing. In addition, root gardens, rock falls, and lesser-maintained treads can make for challenging hiking in sections.

EPIC: Only a few of the hikes in this book have been rated five peaks. They are all over 12 miles long and have elevation gains of more than 4,000 feet. But it's not just the distance and elevation gain that add up to a five-peak rating. These routes may have dangerous river crossings, difficult scrambles, easy-to-lose trails, or some other hardscrabble difficulty. Only experienced, extremely fit hikers should attempt these epics.

Hike Statistics

Distance

This information is given in miles, along with the hike's format, which is listed as loop, out and back, one-way, or lollipop loop.

Elevation

You'll find the hike's low point, high point, and cumulative elevation gain here. Note that I haven't included a simple gain, which is easy for you to calculate on your own. Instead, I have included a cumulative gain that accounts for all of the route's ups. This makes it easier to compare hikes.

Hike Time

Hikers walk anywhere from one and a half to three and a half miles per hour, depending on the difficulty of the tread and the elevation gain. Use the range I provide as a guideline, then consider your own pace, stamina, rest breaks, and map-reading skills to estimate your own time on the trail. Remember that trail conditions and weather can also drastically alter the time it takes to complete a hike. Always call ahead for current trail and weather conditions.

Travel

Notes the driving distance from Seattle.

Season

This entry lists the best time of year to be out on this trail.

Maps

Supplementary maps are extremely helpful, unless you enjoy bivouacking. Most hikes include Green Trails maps recommendations.

Restrictions

It's here you'll find out about restrictions for a given trail—permits, fees, fires, camping, dogs. At most National Forest trailheads, for instance, you need a Northwest Forest Pass or you're likely to get a ticket. Since restrictions are constantly changing, it's smart to call the managing agency for current trail conditions and restrictions.

More Info

The agency that manages the trail is named, and a phone number and website address are also provided. For current trail conditions, maintenance schedule, snow level, permit information, and other restrictions, call ahead.

Trail Notes

Each hike begins with a descriptive overview.

Driving Directions

This paragraph provides detailed instructions for driving to the trailhead. In most cases, I have indicated a point at which you should set the trip odometer in your car to zero.

The Hike

In addition to notes about the terrain, and an occasional quip, The Hike section contains a detailed description of the route—up or down, left or right—and calls out significant landmarks. These paragraphs note the mileage points—in bold—for most intersections, hills, and vistas. The following is an annotated listing of some of the conventions I use when describing the trails.

Confusing or dangerous areas

Whoa! signifies a dangerous section of trail or a turn easily missed, and generally warns you to pay attention.

Oof! (as in, I'm out of breath) identifies the end of a difficult climb.

Stay on the main trail/road, whether in the driving directions or the description of the hike, means that other trails or roads may exit from the main route—use good judgment to continue on the primary trail or road.

In areas with a maze of trails, it's sometimes difficult to figure out which way to go. In these instances, I'll likely mention the **problematic route-finding**.

Forks in the road

When the trail dead-ends at another trail, forcing a 90-degree turn either right or left, the resulting three-way intersection is described as a **T**. Other three-way intersections are usually described as **forks**, though sometimes I write that the **trail divides**. If a **faint trail** or **lesser trail** forks off the main trail, I will sometimes tell you to ignore, pass , or bypass it rather than describe it as a fork. When two trails or roads cross, the result is usually referred to as a **four-way intersection**.

Roads and trails

There are a number of different types of trails and roads described in this book. **Trails** are usually narrow, dirt paths through the woods. A **wide trail**, dirt unless specifically identified as paved, refers to a path 3 to 6 feet wide. A **dirt** or **gravel road** could be used by a car. Roads in National Forests are

On the way to Upper Palisades Lake, Hike 69

usually identified by a number preceded by **FR** for Forest Road, for instance FR 2565. Old roads, sometimes referred to as **doubletracks**, describe narrow, rough roads and may be either motorized or nonmotorized. Sometimes these old roads are gated to keep out motor vehicles. Old railroad grades, or **rail-trails**, are abandoned railroad lines that have no tracks or ties. Typically, rail-trails have the look and feel of dirt roads, although rail-trails are almost always flat and nonmotorized. None of the rail-trails in this book is paved.

Option

For some hikes, I have provided directions to modify the route, bail out early, extend the trip, bag a peak, or catch a nice view.

Gazetteer

Each hike concludes with information on nearby campgrounds and services. The information on the nearest town helps pinpoint the hike's location, identify the nearest gas station, and tell you which direction to head to satisfy your Ben & Jerry's craving. Use the information under Gazetteer to plan a series of weekend day hikes.

Notes

Here's your chance to start a hike diary. Go wild.

THE MAPS

I recorded the mileages and elevation data for each hike using an altimeter, USGS topographic maps, a Global Positioning System (GPS) receiver, and a bunch of note cards and Sharpies. I worked with the data and notes to write the text and create the maps for this guide.

The maps are easy to use, helpful when selecting a hike, and nice to look at. There should be a flow to them that helps tell the story of the trail. With the GPS receiver, I recorded the twists and turns of each hike. Afterward, I downloaded those twists and turns to my computer, and used the data to create a map. So they're accurate as well as being easy to use.

Additional map features: The start and finish of each hike are clearly visible, and the highlighted route prevents map face—squinted eyes and a furrowed brow. Arrows indicate the direction of travel, and intermediary trail mileages are noted between the triangular waypoints. Key elevations are highlighted, and elevation profiles accompany every map. The micro legend helps you make sense of it all, and it's right there, attached to every map.

GPS FEATURES

The most unique (and certainly high tech) map feature is the set of GPS coordinates (waypoints). I used a GPS receiver to make a series of waypoints—an exact location in the latitude / longitude grid—for each hike. Waypoints, marked on each map by a series of numbered triangles, note key junctures along the way. The latitude and longitude coordinates corresponding to each waypoint are found in a small box, usually located in the upper corner of the map.

Three waypoints

The waypoint numbers are latitude and longitude (WGS 84 map datum; dd°mm.mmm format). The latitude and longitude coordinates listed for Waypoint 1 △ represent the precise location of the trailhead, the beginning and end of the route (unless it's a one-way hike). If you have a GPS receiver, you can use the waypoint data by punching the latitude and longitude coordinates listed on each map into your receiver the night before your hike. The following day, your receiver will point toward each successive waypoint for the entire loop, and tell you where you are in relation to the other waypoints.

LEAVE NO TRACE

For the most part hikers do a good job picking up after themselves. But don't be careless—even the smallest piece of a Cliff Shot wrapper can ruin a pristine hike for someone else. But leaving no trace is a bigger job than simply getting all your wrappers stuffed back into your pack. It begins with a quiet and gentle attitude toward the wilderness.

Of course, the worst damage comes from camping and fire building. Camp in designated spots only, well away from lakes and streams. Try to use a stove even where fires are permitted because dead wood has become too scarce. If you do build a fire, always use an existing fire ring.

What Else

- Don't cut switchbacks or hike off the trail.
- Don't widen the trail—stay on the trail even if it's muddy or root-strewn.
- Pick up other people's litter along the way.
- Pick up after your dogs, and don't bring them if they're not allowed.
- Respect other trail users.
- Always respect wildlife—you are in their home!
- Read a book on no-impact hiking.

HIKING TIPS

Eating

It took me a long time to really understand how important it was to eat enough while out on the trail. Don't skimp on calories. Eat a lot or the joy of the hike will end with a dull thud. Eating properly—in other words, constantly—during a hike is more important than training. I'm not just talking about a nice lunch at the lake. On three-peak hikes and longer, I usually start out with at least 1,500 calories of food in my pack (in addition to lunch): candy bars, energy bars, peanuts, Fig Newtons, whatever adds calories to my stomach. Also, don't forget to also include an extra stash of food at the bottom of your pack in the remote chance you spend an unplanned night in the woods.

Drinking

Always bring plenty of water and electrolyte replacement and drink constantly. Two quarts a day is the minimum. I've quaffed two gallons of liquid on really long, hot days. Drinking enough can get you over a lot of hills and get you home before dark. In stark terms: drink or die.

Kids

Learning to hike on Rampart Ridge

Hiking with kids is a joy and a challenge. You'll have to discover that delicate balance between knowing when it's time for a gentle push and knowing when it's time to turn around, even if you haven't made it to the lake. If you're carrying the proper food and gear, though, you'd be surprised at how up for a long hike kids can be. Taking kids out into the woods is also an education, and not just for them. They'll point out all sorts of things you've missed or ignored. Children can help you see the outdoors in fresh and unexpected ways. In the table of contents sorted by difficulty, I've noted some of the easier, flatter hikes that should work for kids. But don't let the suggestions limit you or, more importantly, your kids.

Training

Do some. I guarantee you'll have a better time if you've done some conditioning before heading out. At a minimum, long neighborhood walks and stair climbs with a light pack. More importantly, select the hike and your hiking partner with care. Don't head out on an epic with an über-hiker if you're only in shape for a three-peak jaunt.

Insects

During the summer in the Cascades, flies and mosquitoes can be a real nuisance. Make sure to carry repellant. The only alternative is to keep moving, which helps with the bugs but may scuttle that quiet moment on a rock you'd looked forward to all week. The bugs are less bad immediately after the snow melts and then again after the first hard freeze, usually sometime in September, and those are good times to head out if you're particularly sensitive. For details, call the ranger station and ask about the bug status report.

Theft

Car prowls at trailheads are very common. And it doesn't much matter if it's a secluded trailhead or not. While theft is more of an issue for hikers staying overnight, car break-ins occur even in the middle of the day. Keep this in mind and don't leave anything in your car that you really want when you get back.

FEES

Fees, like insects and thieves, are part of a recreationalist's landscape. To park your car at most **National Forest trailheads**, you need a Northwest Forest Pass. NW Forest Passes, which come in day-pass or yearly-pass varieties, are available at outdoor retailers in the city, ranger stations or country groceries closer to the trailheads. You're likely to get a ticket if you park at a National Forest trailhead without a NW Forest Pass. **Mount Rainier National Park** has long charged an entrance fee. A permit is also required if you want to camp in the national park backcountry. **Washington State Parks** are new to the fee racket. Beginning in 2003, a Natural Investment Vehicle Parking Permit will be required at most state park trailheads. You can buy a day pass or a yearly pass from state park rangers or online. You can also just leave the fee in the metal boxes that have been installed at many state park trailheads. So far the **Washington State Department of Natural Resources** and **King County Parks** do not charge a fee to park at trailheads or walk on the trails.

SAFETY

I've never spent a cold, unplanned night under a tree, knock on wood. But I've read the news reports. And while sometimes getting lost in the dark becomes fodder for a good story (I've got plenty of those), there are many getting-lost stories that don't turn out so well. Be smart and prepared. And remember, being safe isn't only about not getting lost. A twisted ankle or swollen river can easily add a day to your trip, or shorten your life. Use these lists to help plan a safe trip.

Before You Leave

- Find out if the trail has been maintained recently.
- Ask about the condition of the trail.
- Where's the snow level?
- Is it hunting season?
- Check out mountain weather at the National Weather Service website.
- Let someone know where you plan to hike.

Where to Call

King County Parks	206-296-4232
Mount Baker-Snoqualmie National Forest	
Snoqualmie Ranger District (Enumclaw)	360-825-6585
Snoqualmie Ranger District (North Bend)	425-888-1421
Darrington Ranger District (Darrington)	360-436-1155
Darrington Ranger District (Verlot)	360-691-7791
Skykomish District	360-677-2414
Mount Rainier National Park	360-569-2211
National Weather Service	www.wrh.noaa.gov/seattle
Washington State Department of Natural Resources	
Northwest Region	360-856-3500
South Puget Sound Region	360-825-1631
Washington State Parks	360-902-8844
Wenatchee National Forest	
Cle Elum Ranger District	509-674-4411
Lake Wenatchee/Leavenworth District	509-763-3103

Hiking along Gold Creek toward Alaska Lake (see Hike 28)

During the Hike

- If you hike alone, hike with care.
- Drink at least two quarts of water per day. Don't count on finding water.
- Carry a first-aid kit.
- Carry extra clothes and a hat, no matter how nice the weather seems.
- Pack sunscreen, a lighter, a pocket knife, lots of extra food, and a flashlight.
- Carry a map of the area and bring a compass.

Hike 1 ⛰️ ⛰️ ⛰️

WILDERNESS PEAK

Distance	**6.2-mile lollipop loop** (4-mile option)
Elevation	Low point: 400 ft., high point: 1,600 ft., **cumulative gain: 1,750 ft.**
Hike Time	3 to 4 hours, day hike
Travel	18 miles from Seattle
Season	Year round
Map	Green Trails: *Cougar Mountain/Squak Mountain 203S*
Restrictions	Day use only, dogs on leash
More Info	King County Parks, 206-296-4232, www.metrokc.gov/parks/

Trail Notes

Like the mottled bark of the red alder that's common to many of Cougar Mountain's hillsides and slopes, draws and swales, this trail system varies from dirt road to narrow footpath. This route, up Wilderness Creek and around Shy Bear Marsh, takes advantage of some of the best narrow and wild trails on Cougar's south side. The winding trail, twisted and gnarled in sections, passes from the light shade of alder forest to the heavy shade of coniferous forest and back again. While the climb to start the hike is strenuous, much of the rest of the route rolls along the gently contoured pockets of Cougar Mountain's broad top. This loop is more difficult than either the hike to De Leo Wall or the walk from Anti-Aircraft Peak, but it's wilder too.

A trillium in the forest

Driving Directions

Take Interstate 90 eastbound to Exit 15. From the end of the exit ramp, set your odometer to zero and turn right on State Highway 900, which soon becomes the Renton–Issaquah Road. At 3.3 miles, find the small parking area for Wilderness Creek Trailhead on the right.

The Hike

From the parking area, the trail heads up the steep draw along Wilderness Creek. Red alder dominate the hillside, with the occasional red cedar. Just after crossing the creek, reach a T in the trail at **0.5 mile** and turn

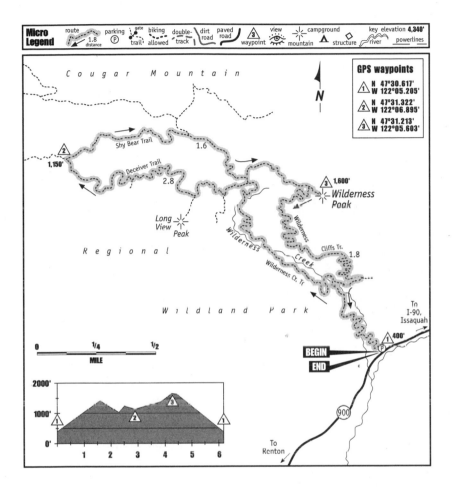

Micro Legend — route 1.8 distance | parking ℗ | gate | biking trail | double-track | dirt road | paved road | 3 waypoint | view mountain | campground structure | key elevation 4,340' | powerlines | river

GPS waypoints

1️⃣ N 47°30.617'
W 122°05.205'

2️⃣ N 47°31.322'
W 122°06.895'

3️⃣ N 47°31.213'
W 122°05.603'

Cougar Mountain

Regional Wildland Park

Shy Bear Trail 1.6
Deceiver Trail 2.8
Long View Peak
Wilderness Peak 1,600'
Wilderness Creek
Wilderness Cr. Tr.
Cliffs Tr. 1.8
1,150'
400'
900
To I-90, Issaquah
To Renton

BEGIN
END

left. The trail crosses the creek again and continues up. Around **1.0 mile**, the trail levels for a spell to meander across the marshy headwaters of Wilderness Creek. At **1.6 miles**, reach a T in the trail and turn left on S4, toward Long View Peak. **Oof!** The difficult climb is now complete.

At **1.7 miles**, ignore Trail S5 on the left. When you reach a fork in the trail at **2.0 miles**, bear right on Deceiver Trail S3. From here, the trail descends easily through a hemlock and Douglas fir forest, with an occasional cedar. Below in a large depression to the right, Shy Bear Marsh, studded with tall alder, gives an airy feeling to the landscape. At **2.3 miles**, reach a fork and bear right. (Find Doughty Falls one-tenth of a mile down to the left.) From here, Deceiver Trail continues

25

west, climbing over a broad hump before descending. At **2.8 miles**, reach a fork and turn right on Shy Bear Trail S2.

From here, the trail heads east. You'll cross a series of boardwalks over rich muck and skunk cabbage as you traverse the boggy north side of Shy Bear Marsh.

At **3.4 miles**, reach a fork and bear right, continuing on Shy Bear Trail toward Shy Bear Pass. Reach a T in the trail at **3.8 miles**—Shy Bear Pass—and turn left. The trail, narrow and wild, climbs steeply toward Wilderness Peak. At **4.2 miles**, reach a fork and bear left. The top of the peak is a few short bends in the trail farther. From the top, turn around and retrace your steps back to the fork, now **4.4 miles**. Turn left and begin down Wilderness Cliffs Trail, which is steep and rootstrewn. Several spur trails jog off the main trail, affording middling views into the treetops to the south. At **5.7 miles**, reach a fork and turn left. Cross the bridge over Wilderness Creek and descend back to the parking area at **6.2 miles**.

Spring arrives near Wilderness Peak

Option

From the T at 1.6 miles, turn right, following the sign toward Wilderness Peak. A few strides down the trail, ignore another trail that forks off to the left. From here, follow the description above, beginning from the 3.8-mile mark. This optional route shrinks the lollipop loop to 4 miles.

Gazetteer

Nearby camping: Denny Creek Campground

Nearest food, drink, services: Issaquah

NOTES:

_____

_____

_____

_____

Hike 2 ⛰ ⛰
DE LEO WALL

Distance	5-mile loop
Elevation	Low point: 650 ft.; high point: 1,120 ft.; **cumulative gain: 1,100 ft.**
Hike Time	2 to 4 hours, day hike
Travel	16 miles from Seattle
Season	Year round
Map	Green Trails: *Cougar Mountain / Squak Mountain 203S*
Restrictions	Day use only, dogs on leash
More Info	King County Parks, 206-296-4232, www.metrokc.gov/parks/

Trail Notes

Lots of turns, forks, and intersections on this route, but the trails at Cougar Mountain are well signed. The highlights are the surprising remoteness and the view from De Leo Wall through the tops of madrone trees. While most of this route is easy walking, a couple of strenuous climbing sections require a modicum of agility, maybe two. The parking area is fairly big, but Red Town is Cougar's most popular trailhead, and it can be crowded on good-weather weekends.

Driving Directions

From Seattle, go east on Interstate 90 to Exit 13. When the ramp splits, bear right toward Lakemont. Zero out your odometer at the end of the exit ramp and turn right onto Lakemont Boulevard S.E. Stay on the arterial as it winds up and over the hill. At 3.1 miles, turn left into Cougar Mountain Regional Wildland Park's Red Town Trailhead. Park in the lot on the right.

The Hike

Whoa! Four trails begin from Red Town Trailhead. Those trails, in turn, fork off in an ever larger maze of trails, both narrow and wide, so following a particular route can be difficult. As you drive into the trailhead and bear to the right, you'll see two gates. The trail to De Leo Wall begins on Wildside Trail W1, which starts beyond the left of the two gates near the kiosk. Two trails begin here; Wildside is the one on the right.

Take Wildside Trail toward De Leo Wall. At **0.1 mile**, bear right at the fork and cross over a short bridge. At **0.15 mile**, Wildside Trail jogs left: Turn left at

27

the T and then immediately turn right to continue on W1. At **0.2 mile**, reach a T and turn right to remain on Wildside Trail. There are two forks at the **0.3-mile** mark—bear left at the first and right at the second to remain on W1. You've now completed the most difficult part of the hike—route-finding the first half-mile.

Reach a fork at **0.7 mile** and turn right on Marshall Hill Trail W6. From here the trail switchbacks up the hill. At **0.9 mile**, bear right at the fork and continue up. With the switchbacks complete, reach a fork at **1.1 miles** and bear left, following the rolls of the uneven hillside. The trail forks two more times over the next half-mile—bear left each time to stay on W6.

Cross a paved, one-lane road at **1.8 miles**. Across the road the trail becomes De Leo Wall Trail W9. When the trail forks at **1.9 miles**, turn left, pass through the wood stile, and begin climbing again. At **2.1 miles**, pass over the top of the

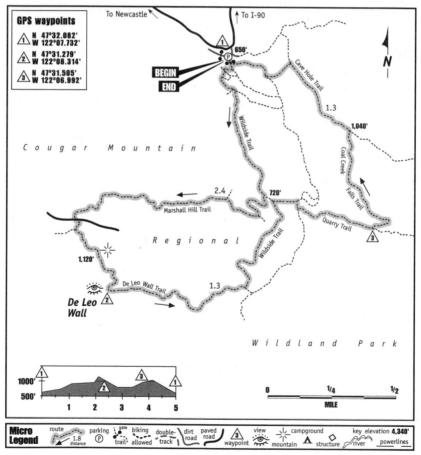

hill and descend steeply. The trail, narrow and peppered with roots, winds through a conifer forest that includes madrone, salal, and Oregon grape. At **2.4 miles**, reach a viewpoint from the top of De Leo Wall.

From here, De Leo Wall Trail W9 continues a melodious descent, riffing eastward around the south flank of Marshall Hill. At **2.8 miles**, reach a fork and bear left on Wildside Trail W1. The trail rolls through the forest here, climbing and descending. At a fork, **3.3 miles**, turn right. At **3.4 miles**, turn right again. Almost immediately reach another fork. This time bear left on Quarry Trail C6 toward Coal Creek Falls. The trail quickly begins climbing. At **3.7 miles**, turn left on Coal Creek Falls Trail C4. The trail drops and winds to the falls, which are small and sweet. Cross the creek and traverse north, climbing gently. The trail is lovely here, narrow and intimate.

Reach the junction with Cave Hole Trail C3 at **4.2 miles**. Turn left and walk down this wide trail. At **4.6 miles**, reach a fork and bear left, continuing on C3. At **4.8 miles**, reach a fork and bear right on Red Town Trail. The trail continues descending until you reach the trailhead parking area, **5.0 miles**.

Gazetteer

Nearby camping. Denny Creek Campground

Nearest food, drink, services: Issaquah

NOTES:

6/21/08 - Lee & Bri w/ variations

Hike 3 ⛰

ANTI-AIRCRAFT PEAK

Distance	3.7-mile lollipop loop
Elevation	Low point: 1,180 ft.; high point: 1,470 ft.; **cumulative gain: 600 ft.**
Hike Time	1 to 3 hours, day hike
Travel	18 miles from Seattle
Season	Year round
Map	Green Trails: *Cougar Mountain/Squak Mountain 203S*
Restrictions	Day use only, dogs on leash
More Info	King County Parks, 206-296-4232, www.metrokc.gov/parks/

Trail Notes

Cougar Mountain is a beautiful, if enigmatic, place. In addition to some big guns, Anti-Aircraft Peak Trailhead was once, not really too long ago, an active Nike Missile Launch Site. It seems hard to swallow these days. For much of the last century, the mountain was logged and mined, prodded, poked, and explored. Mine shafts, faintly terraced roadbeds, and rusted cables remain from the intrusions. Even today, a wide road winds up to an active clay pit on the mountain. Yet now Cougar is the centerpiece of the King County Parks system, as alder, cedar, and fir have reclaimed the rangy, rolling land between Newcastle and Issaquah. This is an easy hike and a great introduction to the mountain; it has longer and shorter options, and the elevation gain is minimal.

Driving Directions

From Seattle, go east on Interstate 90 to Exit 13. When the exit ramp splits, bear right toward Lakemont. Zero out your odometer at the end of the ramp and turn right onto Lakemont Boulevard S.E. Stay on the arterial as it winds up and over the hill. At 2.4 miles, turn left on S.E. Cougar Mountain Way, which as you go up becomes first 168th Place S.E., and then S.E. 60th Street. At 3.6 miles,

reach a fork and bear right on S.E. Cougar Mountain Drive. At 4.5 miles, reach a fork and bear right again, entering Cougar Mountain Park. At 4.8 miles, reach the trailhead and park.

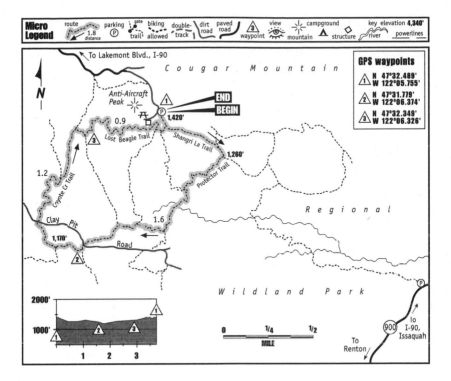

The Hike

From the parking area at Anti-Aircraft Peak Trailhead, take Shangri La Trail E1. Reach a fork in the trail at **0.1 mile** and bear left, continuing along Shangri La Trail. The trail, wide and lined with red alder, gently descends in an open clockwise curve around the eastern shoulder of Anti-Aircraft Peak. At **0.4 mile**, ignore a trail on the left. Just beyond, reach another fork and bear right on Protector Trail E9, heading toward Tibbetts Marsh Trail. Unlike the predictable curving path of Shangri La, Protector Trail twists and turns as it negotiates cedar and fir roots and small alder blowdown.

At **0.8 mile**, reach a T and turn left on N9. Immediately west of the T you'll find Tibbetts Marsh, a sea of tall alder. The trail meanders around the south side of the marsh, past a number of huge stumps topped by wigs of salal. Cross a log bridge over a small Tibbetts Creek tributary. Reach a T in the trail at **1.2 miles** and turn right, toward Cougar Pass.

At **1.4 miles**, reach Cougar Pass. Ignore the trail on the right and continue on Cougar Pass Trail. At **1.5 miles**, reach a T and turn left on Klondike Swamp Trail N5. At **1.7 miles**, cross Clay Pit Road to Fred's Railroad Trail. Almost immedi-

Shangri La Trail near Anti-Aircraft Peak

ately, the trail forks—turn right on Clay Pit Bypass Trail. Descend through a small stand of cedar and cross the North Fork of Coal Creek.

The trail ascends slightly after the creek, then widens. Reach a fork at **1.9 miles** and bear right, walking along a wide doubletrack. Cross Clay Pit Road again. After crossing the road, pick up Coyote Creek Trail. At **2.5 miles**, pass by a trail on the left to Radio Peak. From here the trail edges along the western slope of Klondike Marsh. At **2.8 miles**, reach a fork and turn right. The trail quickly drops, crosses Coal Creek, then bends to the right. **Whoa!** Watch out for the fork at **2.9 miles**: Take a hard left on Lost Beagle Trail. This narrow, easily missed trail climbs steadily, winding through a deep conifer forest peppered with alder—perhaps the most beautiful section of the route. After the climb, the way eases along for a time. Pass an unexpected fence on the left. At **3.5 miles**, reach a T and turn left. Quickly reach another T and turn left again. At **3.6 miles**, reach a T at Shangri La Trail and turn left. Reach the parking area at **3.7 miles**.

Gazetteer

Nearby camping: Denny Creek Campground
Nearest food, drink, services: Issaquah

NOTES:

_____

_____

_____

_____

Hike 4 ⛰ ⛰ ⛰
BEAR RIDGE

Distance	7.5-mile lollipop loop
Elevation	Low point: 220 ft., high point: 1,460 ft., **cumulative gain: 1,700 ft.**
Hike Time	3 to 5 hours, day hike
Travel	18 miles from Seattle
Season	Year round
Map	Green Trails: *Cougar Mountain/Squak Mountain 203S*
Restrictions	Day use only, dogs on leash
More Info	King County Parks, 206-296-4232, www.metrokc.gov/parks/

Trail Notes

The hike up Cougar Mountain's Bear Ridge feels solitary and peaceful soon after leaving the trailhead. One reason could be the lack of parking at the trailhead: two cars maximum, and this keeps people away. It's also easy to drive past the trailhead without seeing it, and since turning around on State Highway 900 is dangerous, there's probably a lot of "Well, let's just go to the Wilderness Creek Trail instead." Like the history of Cougar Mountain, this route engages, winding past the Fantastic Erratic boulder, past a gated mine shaft, along an old logging railroad grade, and even including the Shangri La Trail.

Driving Directions

Take Interstate 90 eastbound to Exit 15. From the end of the exit ramp, set your odometer to zero and turn right on State Hwy 900, which soon becomes the Renton–Issaquah Road. At 1.4 miles, find the tiny, easily missed parking slot for Bear Ridge Trailhead on the right.

The Hike

The trail seems to originate right from the highway near Issaquah, but with a sleight of hand almost immediately offers the feeling that it's out there in the middle of nowhere. Wide for a hun-

On the way up Bear Ridge

33

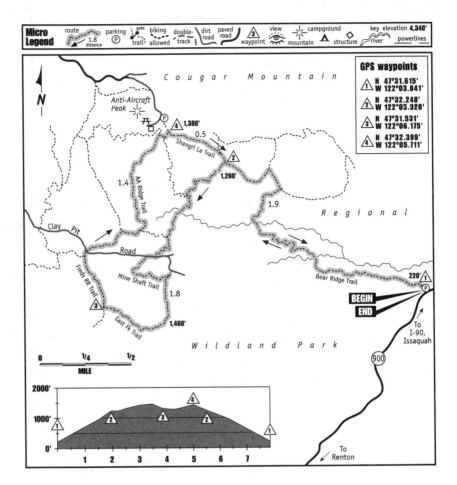

dred yards, the trail forks—bear left on Bear Ridge Trail E3—then narrows and climbs through the alder-and salmonberry-filtered light of east Cougar Mountain. At about **0.7 mile**, pass around the Erratic Fantastic boulder, which is covered in ferns, and continue ascending. At **1.5 miles**, reach a T and begin a series of left turns. Turn left again at **1.6 miles** and at **1.9 miles**, onto the Protector Trail E9, which is narrow and winding. Most of the elevation gain is out of the way, and the trail rolls and swells along the wide top of East Cougar.

At **2.2 miles**, reach a T and turn left onto N9. After crossing a creek that drains from Tibbetts Marsh, reach a fork at **2.5 miles** and head left. The trail climbs to Clay Pit Road—turn right, walk less than 100 yards, then turn left onto Mine Shaft Trail C10. After passing the old gated mine, reach a fork at **3.0 miles**

An old Cougar Mountain mine shaft

and turn right, swinging south and then west on East Fork Trail C8. At **3.7 miles**, reach a T and turn right on Freds Railroad Trail C7. When the trail divides at **4.0 miles**, bear right, then almost immediately cross over Clay Pit Road.

At **4.2 miles**, reach a fork and turn right on Cougar Pass Trail N8. But just up the trail, **4.3 miles**, turn left at the fork onto Anti-Aircraft Ridge Trail. At **5.0 miles**, reach a fork and bear right. In quick succession, turn left and then turn right, following Shangri La Trail E1 and heading away from the Anti-Aircraft Peak Trailhead. Ignore a trail on the left at **5.5 miles**. But when you reach a fork at **5.6 miles**, turn left. From here, turn right at **5.9 miles** and again at **6.0 miles**, reconnecting with Bear Ridge Trail. Follow the trail down to the parking area along State Hwy 900, **7.5 miles**.

Gazetteer

Nearby camping: Denny Creek Campground
Nearest food, drink, services: Issaquah

NOTES:

_____

_____

_____

_____

Hike 5 ⛰️ ⛰️

SQUAK MOUNTAIN

Distance	5.3-mile lollipop loop
Elevation	Low point: 740 ft., high point: 1,930 ft., **cumulative gain: 1,550 ft.**
Hike Time	2 to 4 hours, day hike
Travel	20 miles from Seattle
Season	Year round
Map	Green Trails: *Cougar Mountain/Squak Mountain 203S*
Restrictions	State Parks vehicle fee, day use only, dogs on leash
More Info	Washington State Parks, 360-902-8844, www.parks.wa.gov

Trail Notes

Tucked between Cougar Mountain to the west and Tiger Mountain to the east, both of which sport many trails, Squak Mountain might get an inferiority complex. It doesn't need to. The trails on Squak are less crowded than trails on those other Issaquah Alps, and you can quickly hike to secluded areas. This is a great winter hike, when the days are short and you wait to see what the weather looks like on Saturday morning before deciding to drive out to a trail. This route climbs close to the top of Squak's Central Peak, then later wraps quietly around the dry, south-facing side of West Peak.

Driving Directions

From Seattle, take Interstate 90 east to Exit 17 in Issaquah. At the end of the exit ramp, set your odometer to zero and turn right onto Front Street. At 0.6 mile, turn right on Sunset Way. Proceed straight through the light at 0.8 mile, and go up the steep hill, which becomes Mountain Park Boulevard S.W. Stay on the main road as it winds and climbs. At 1.7 miles, turn left on Mountainside Drive. At 2.1 miles, just before a sweeping switchback to the left, pull into the small, paved parking area straight ahead.

The old Bullitt Fireplace

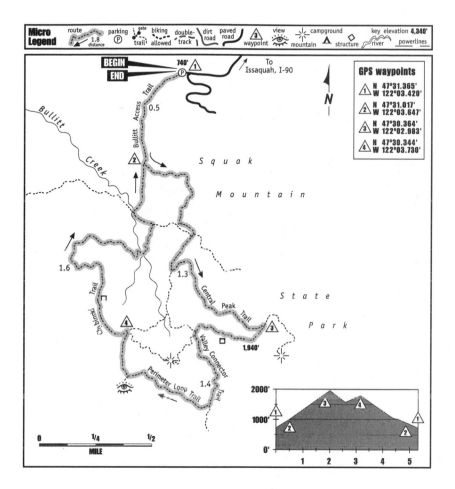

Micro Legend — route / 1.8 distance / parking ℗ / gate biking trail allowed / double-track / dirt road / paved road / ▲₃ waypoint / view / mountain / campground / ▲ structure / river / key elevation **4,340'** powerlines

BEGIN / END

740' ▲₁

To Issaquah, I-90

N

GPS waypoints

▲₁ N 47°31.365'
W 122°03.420'

▲₂ N 47°31.017'
W 122°03.647'

▲₃ N 47°30.364'
W 122°02.983'

▲₄ N 47°30.344'
W 122°03.730'

Bullitt Creek

Bullitt Access Trail

0.5

▲₂

S q u a k

M o u n t a i n

1.6

1.3

Central Peak Trail

Peak

S t a t e

▲₃

P a r k

Chybinski Trail

▲₄

Valley Connector Trail

1,940'

Perimeter Loop Trail

1.4

2000'

1000'

0'

1   2   3   4   5

0   1/4   1/2
MILE

The Hike

From the small trailhead along Mountainside Drive, walk up the wide trail that begins beyond the large rocks. The Bullitt Access Trail N1 curves up the hillside at an easy grade, first through mature and then young alder. At **0.5 mile**, reach a fork and bear left, continuing up N1 toward Central Peak. From here the trail, still climbing steadily, passes through a mature stand of second growth.

At **0.8 mile**, ignore a faint trail on the right. Reach a fork in the trail at **1.0 mile** and bear right. Almost immediately, the trail forks again: Take the left fork, continuing up toward Central Peak. At **1.2 miles**, reach a fork and turn left on Central Peak Trail. After a steep stretch, the trail levels somewhat, and the hillside affords views north toward Issaquah. At **1.8 miles**, reach a fork—turn right. (The left fork climbs to the top of Central Peak, one quarter-mile farther, for a nice view of microwave towers, a cement building, and chain link fences.) The right fork climbs quickly to the high point at **2.0 miles**. Just beyond the high point, you'll pass the old Bullitt Fireplace on the left.

From the fireplace, descend through a dark hemlock and cedar forest. **Whoa!** At **2.2 miles**, reach a fork and turn left onto a faint trail, which is easily missed.

Almost immediately there's another fork: Bear left on West Valley Connector Trail C3. (The trail on the right climbs to the top of West Peak.) Descending, this lonesome trail heads due south, probing the headwaters of Bullitt Creek. At **2.6 miles**, reach a fork and turn right on Perimeter Loop Trail. This long up-hill traverse around the south slope of West Peak follows a narrow, lightly used trail, and the fir and salal forest nicely captures the late afternoon sun.

Pass by a short spur to a viewpoint on the left at **3.0 miles**. At **3.2 miles**, reach a fork and bear left. A few strides farther, reach a T and turn left on Chybinski Trail. After some descending, pass the old blockhouse on the right.

From here the trail winds downward, twisting along Squak Mountain's western slope. At **4.3 miles**, drop down a tight draw and cross a creek. At **4.4 miles**, reach a T and turn left on West Access Trail. Reach a fork in the trail at **4.6 miles** and turn right on Coal Mine Trail, heading toward Mountainside Drive Trailhead. At **4.8 miles**, reach a fork and bear left. Reach the parking area at **5.3 miles**.

Gazetteer
Nearby camping: Denny Creek Campground
Nearest food, drink, services: Issaquah

NOTES:

_____

_____

_____

_____

Hike 6 ⛰ ⛰ ⛰ ⛰

WEST TIGER RAMBLER

Distance	11.2-mile loop
Elevation	Low point: 490 ft., high point: 2,020 ft., **cumulative gain: 2,080 ft.**
Hike Time	4 to 7 hours, day hike
Travel	21 miles from Seattle
Season	Year round
Map	Green Trails: *Tiger Mountain 204S*
Restrictions	Day use only, dogs on leash
More Info	Washington State Department of Natural Resources, South Puget Sound Region, 360-825-1631, www.wa.gov/dnr/

Trail Notes

Tiger Mountain has a wealth of great trails; some are well-signed and well-worn, others are narrow, unsigned tracks. On most you'll find steep climbing. This long loop follows some of the more well known, though often lonesome, trails on West Tiger—the Old Bus Road Trail, Poo Poo Point Trail, West Tiger Railroad Grade, and Tiger Mountain Trail—around two of West Tiger's three summits. The loop engages most of the trail systems on West Tiger, so it's a nice introduction and will make you want to go back and explore.

Driving Directions

From Seattle, take Interstate 90 east to Exit 20. Turn right at the end of the exit ramp, and then immediately turn right again onto S.E. 79th Street toward Tradition Lake Trail. After one-half mile pass through a gate (closed after 8 p.m.). Just short of one mile, reach the High Point Trailhead. It's often crowded, so you may have to park along the paved access road and walk to this point.

The Hike

From the main kiosk near the toilets, follow the sign toward the trails, and immediately bear right at the fork (the group picnic area is on the left). At **0.1 mile**, reach a 4-way intersection and turn left, passing through a wood gate. When the trail forks at **0.2 mile**, bear right on the Bus Road Trail, which is wide and flat. Ignore a trail on the left at **0.4 mile**. Just past the rusted out bus frame—the trail's namesake—reach a fork and bear left. When the trail divides at **1.0 mile**, turn left

39

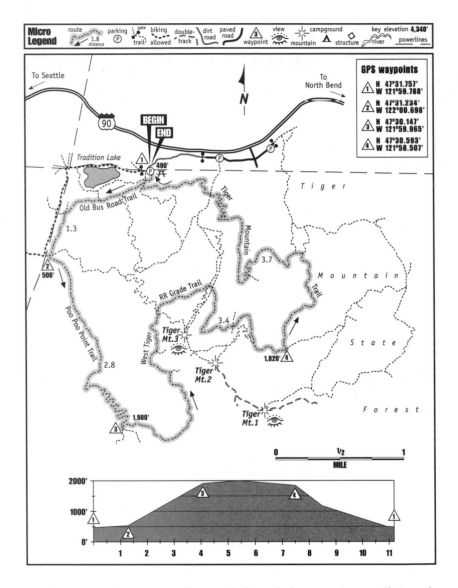

on Gas Line Trail, a narrow, rolling track through the grass. At **1.3 miles**, reach a 4-way and take a gentle left onto the Poo Poo Point Trail.

From here the trail begins a steep climb toward Many Creeks Valley, then above to the high south shoulder of West Tiger's three summits. Around the **2.2-mile** point, you'll traverse into Many Creeks Valley and cross several bridges before ascending again. The final pitch, which stretches for over a mile, is so steep that conversation will cease until the top. **Oof!** Finally, at **4.1 miles**, reach a 4-way intersection and turn left on West Tiger Mountain Railroad Grade. All of the serious climbing is now complete.

The West Tiger Railroad Grade Trail, as its name implies, follows the route of an old logging railroad as it winds almost completely around the summits of West Tiger 2 and West Tiger 3. Though there are some ups and downs, the trail runs mostly level. Just after the **5.0-mile** mark, ignore a trail on the right. At **5.4 miles**, ignore another trail on the right. Reach a 4-way at **5.7 miles**, and continue straight on West Tiger Railroad Grade. At **6.2 miles**, reach another 4-way at the junc-

Making tracks on Tiger

tion with West Tiger 3 Trail and again continue straight. Immediately cross the cable line, used by some as a trail, then continue the winding on a level traverse. Pass straight through yet another 4-way, this one unmarked, then ignore a trail on the right that climbs to the summit of West Tiger 2.

At **7.5 miles**, reach a fork and turn left, descending on Tiger Mountain Trail. The trail drops back into the bright alder and salmonberry; at times the descent is steep. Cross a small creek at Ruth's Cove and follow the trail through a lush and beautiful forest of old-growth red alder, cedar, and Douglas fir. Reach a fork in the trail at **8.4 miles** and bear left. When the trail forks again, bear left, continuing on Tiger Mountain Trail toward the High Point Trailhead. Just beyond, cross a bridge over an eastern channel of High Point Creek and begin climbing again.

Ignore a ragged, unmarked trail on the left. The main trail climbs to around **9.2 miles** then crosses a creek and descends, gradually at first and then quickly. Cross over the cable line. Ignore a trail on the right at **10.7 miles**. At **11.0 miles**, reach a T—turn right. Pass by Old Bus Road Trail on the left. When you reach the wood gate, turn right then left, reaching the trailhead at **11.2 miles**.

Gazetteer
Nearby camping: Denny Creek Campground
Nearest food, drink, services: Issaquah

NOTES:

_____

_____

Hike 7 ⛰ ⛰ ⛰
WEST TIGER MOUNTAIN 3

Distance	5.0-mile out and back
Elevation	Low point: 480 ft., high point: 2,520 ft., **cumulative gain: 2,040 ft.**
Hike Time	2 to 4 hours, day hike
Travel	21 miles from Seattle
Season	Year round
Map	Green Trails: *Tiger Mountain 204S*
Restrictions	Day use only, dogs on leash
More Info	Washington State Department of Natural Resources, South Puget Sound Region, 360-825-1631, www.wa.gov/dnr/

Trail Notes

Tiger Mountain, just southeast of Issaquah, boasts six summits. From the popular High Point Trailhead along Interstate 90, the three summits that comprise West Tiger Mountain—creatively named West Tiger Numbers 1, 2, and 3—are all within pre-lunch striking distance. This route climbs to the top of the closest, lowest, and most popular of the three crests—West Tiger Mountain 3. Many of the trails are heavily used, even on weekdays, so expect to say hello to lots of people, many with their dogs, along the route.

Driving Directions

From Seattle, take Interstate 90 east to Exit 20. Turn right at the end of the exit ramp, and then immediately turn right again on S.E. 79th Street toward Tradition Lake Trail. After one-half mile pass through a white gate (note that it closes at 8pm). Just short of one mile, reach the gravel parking area for High Point Trailhead. This parking area is often full, so you may have to park along the paved access road before the white gate and walk to the trailhead.

The Hike

From the main kiosk near the toilets, follow the sign toward the trails, and immediately bear right at the fork (the group picnic area is on the left). At **0.1 mile**, reach a 4-way intersection and turn left, passing through a wood fence. When the trail forks at **0.2 mile**, bear left on West Tiger 3 Trail. Just beyond this

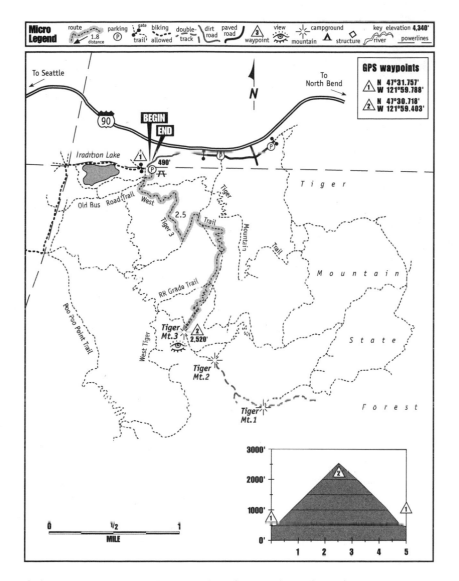

fork, ignore an unmarked trail on the left. From here, the wide, sometimes gravelly trail climbs steeply through a forest of red alder.

At **0.8 mile**, reach a fork and bear left. The trail is narrower here and still steep. After several more uphill twists, West Tiger 3 Trail parallels a cable line corridor that runs straight up West Tiger Mountain. Signs discourage use of this

Up West Tiger 3

wide, ugly, steep, and unmaintained route to the top, so stick with the official trail—West Tiger 3. After crossing the cable corridor several more times, reach a 4-way intersection at **2.0 miles**—continue straight on West Tiger 3, continuing the difficult climb. Gradually during the climb the red alder and fern forest give way to a mix of fir, hemlock, and salal.

The trail crosses the cable line again and then kisses it as the two routes closely parallel each other up the final ridge to the summit of West Tiger Mountain 3, **2.5 miles**. Oof! Take in the outstanding views of the distant Seattle skyline, Tiger Mountain 2, and Mount Rainier in the distance. From the top, retrace your steps to the trailhead parking.

Gazetteer

Nearby camping: Denny Creek Campground

Nearest food, drink, services: Issaquah

NOTES:

_____

_____

_____

_____

Hike 8 ⛰️ ⛰️
TALUS ROCKS ✓

Distance	3.3-mile loop
Elevation	Low point: 520 ft., high point: 1,140 ft., **cumulative gain: 700 ft.**
Hike Time	2 to 3 hours, day hike
Travel	21 miles from Seattle
Season	Year round
Map	Green Trails. *Tiger Mountain 204S*
Restrictions	Day use only, dogs on leash
More Info	Washington State Department of Natural Resources, South Puget Sound Region, 360-825-1631, www.wa.gov/dnr/

Trail Notes

The loop to the Talus Rocks and back via Nook Trail is beautiful and entertaining. The rocks—huge, dark, mysteriously caved, and covered in fern—are the highlight. Since this trail short and the elevation gain modest, it's a relatively popular loop, though the steep first mile will take it out of you.

Driving Directions

From Seattle, take Interstate 90 east to Exit 20. Turn right at the end of the exit ramp, and then immediately turn right again onto S.E. 79th Street toward Tradition Lake Trail. After one-half mile pass through a white gate (closed after 8pm). Just short of one mile, reach the gravel parking area for High Point Trailhead. This trailhead is often crowded, so you may have to park along the paved access road and walk to the trailhead.

Fern and talus rocks

The Hike

From the main kiosk near the toilets, follow the sign toward the trails. Immediately bear right at the fork (the group picnic area is on the left). At **0.1 mile**, reach a 4-way intersection and turn left, passing through a wood gate. When the trail forks at **0.2 mile**, bear left on West Tiger 3. Pass by a trail on the left. After a bend, the trail begins a steep ascent through a forest of red alder, devil's club, salmonberry, and fern.

45

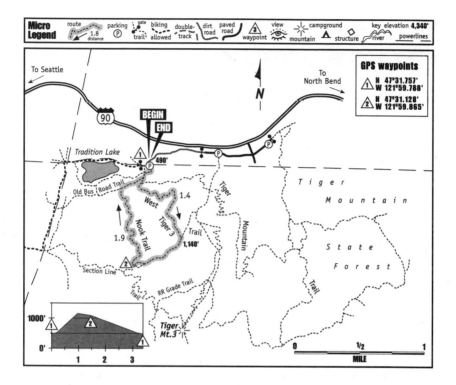

Reach a fork at **1.0 mile** and turn right on Connector Trail. From here, the way traverses the steep north flank of West Tiger 3. At **1.4 miles**, reach the Talus Rocks. Numerous exploratory trails flow around the rocks and then head off toward Section Line Trail to the west. For this loop, stay to the right, connecting with Nook Trail just below the rocks. Nook Trail descends into a lovely ferned valley, heading due north. Around the **2.2-mile** mark, the trail meets a small creek and runs parallel to it. Reach a T at **2.9 miles** and turn right onto the Old Bus Road Trail. At **3.1 miles**, bear left at the fork. Return to the trailhead parking area at **3.3 miles**.

Gazetteer

Nearby camping: Denny Creek Campground
Nearest food, drink, services: Issaquah

NOTES:

Hike 9 ⛰ ⛰ ⛰
DWIGHT'S WAY

Distance	5.4-mile lollipop loop
Elevation	Low point: 520 ft., high point: 2,120 ft., **cumulative gain: 1,850 ft.**
Hike Time	3 to 4 hours, day hike
Travel	21 miles from Seattle
Season	Year round
Map	Green Trails: *Tiger Mountain 204S*
Restrictions	Day use only, dogs on leash
More Info	Washington State Department of Natural Resources, South Puget Sound Region, 360-825-1631, www.wa.gov/dnr/

Trail Notes
I wanted to title this hike Lingering Loop, after the trail by the same name, because of its lonesome, winding, almost forgetful nature. As it stands now, though, time has forgotten parts of that trail. So I settled on Dwight's Way, one of the trails along the route which is narrow, delicate, lovely, and it embodies the spirit of Lingering Loop, if not the name. Brushy, steep, and remote (for Tiger Mountain, at least), this is a difficult loop, despite the moderate distance.

Driving Directions
From Seattle, take Interstate 90 east to Exit 20. Turn right at the end of the exit ramp, and then immediately turn left on S.E. 79th Street, heading away from Tradition Lake Trail. The road ends at a turnaround in one quarter-mile.

The Hike
From the turnaround, hike out the trail that begins beyond the white gate. Pass by a tiny pond on the right. Just past the pond, reach a fork and turn right. The trail climbs sharply for a short distance to a T. Turn right at the T and continue ascending through maple and red alder, with the rush of I-90 still in your ears. At **0.4 mile**, pass under a set of power lines, then through a wood gate, continuing a steady climb into a darker, richer forest where the steep valley and High Point Creek well below on the right gradually obscure the intrusive noise of the interstate.

When the trail forks at **0.8 mile**, turn left onto Dwight's Way. **Whoa!** This is an easy turn to miss. At **0.9 miles**, reach a fork and bear left. From here, Dwight's Way, narrow and mossy, traverses eastward, twisting in and out of the folds of Tiger Mountain. This is a quiet and absolutely lovely section. The trail divides at **1.5 miles**—turn right and immediately begin a steep climb up a narrow trail. This leg of the hike can be wet, brushy, and covered with spider webs.

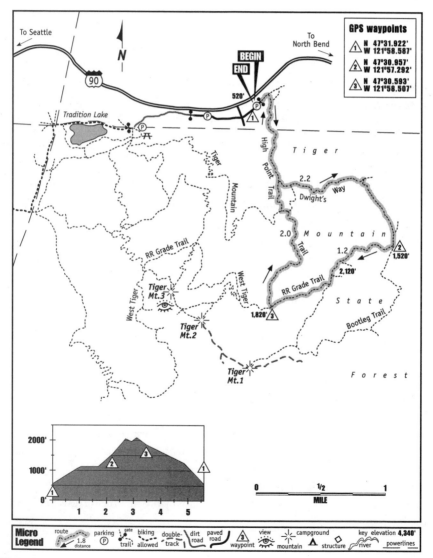

At **2.0 miles**, reach a fork and bear right. When the trail forks again at **2.1 miles**, bear right. From here, the trail again pushes the upper limits of steep climbing, angling southwest to a high point at **2.6 miles**. Pass by two trails on the left, one just before the crest and one just after. The way climbs again to another fork at **2.8 miles**—turn right on West Tiger Railroad Grade toward the Tiger Mountain Trail. From here, the trail heads mostly downhill toward the junction with Tiger Mountain Trail.

At **3.3 miles**, reach a fork and turn right on Tiger Mountain Trail, signed TMT. The trail descends sharply, finally crossing a creek in a dark hollow, before rolling then dropping again to a fork at **4.2 miles**. Bear left to remain on Tiger Mountain Trail. When the trail divides again at **4.3 miles**, turn right. At **4.5 miles**, ignore a trail on the right and continue descending. Cross under a set of power lines at **4.9 miles**. At **5.2 miles**, turn left at the fork, drop for a short distance, then turn left again. Reach the parking area at **5.3 miles**.

Picking flowers on Tiger Mountain

Gazetteer

Nearby camping: Denny Creek Campground

Nearest food, drink, services: Issaquah

NOTES:

_____

_____

_____

_____

Hike 10 ⛰ ⛰ ⛰ ⛰

RATTLESNAKE MOUNTAIN

Distance	**7.2-mile out and back**
Elevation	Low point: 900 ft., high point: 3,480 ft., **cumulative gain: 2,700 ft.**
Hike Time	4 to 7 hours, day hike
Travel	35 miles from Seattle
Season	May through October
Map	Green Trails: *Rattlesnake Mountain 205S*
Restrictions	Day use only, dogs on leash
More Info	Washington State Department of Natural Resources, South Puget Sound Region, 360-825-1631, www.wa.gov/dnr/

Trail Notes

The climb up to Rattlesnake Ledge is steep and root-strewn, through a dark conifer forest without much in the way of undergrowth. Since it's close to Seattle and only a mile and a half to the rocky cliffs and lookouts that afford long views of the South Fork of the Snoqualmie River valley, it's also quite popular. But the trail continues climbing above those crags, which are dotted blue, red, and bright green from the packs and fleece and foggy-day shells, all the way up to the east and west summits of Rattlesnake Mountain, more of a broad ridge than mountain. Above the ledge, the trail continues just as steep and barely six inches wide in places, brushy with salal and young firs, until it reaches an old forest road that leads to the summit. It's a tough climb and the route to the top is a little confusing, but there aren't many people up there and the views are terrific.

Driving Directions

From Seattle, take Interstate 90 east to Exit 32. At the end of the interstate ramp, zero out your odometer and turn right onto 436th Avenue S.E. This becomes Cedar Falls Road S.E. Stay on the main road. At 3.1 miles, reach the parking area for Rattlesnake Ledge Trail on the right. Note: There's additional parking at Rattlesnake Lake, further up on the right, and Iron Horse State Park and the Snoqualmie Valley Trail further up on the left.

The Hike

The trail begins beyond a white gate on an old roadbed. Follow the signs for Rattlesnake Mountain Trail as you wind through lowland at the northeast end of Rattlesnake Lake. The forest is mixed here, with alder, fir, and hemlock. After rounding the end of the lake, **0.3 mile**, the trail abruptly bears right and begins ascending the southern end of Rattlesnake Mountain. Wide and root-strewn, the newly rebuilt trail stairsteps up the slope, leaving the lake behind.

The route up offers no pause or respite, and you may find yourself clinging to a tree to regain balance from the dizzying ascent. **Oof!** After climbing 1,100 feet in slightly more than one mile, reach a T at Rattlesnake Ledge, **1.6 miles**. Turn left and continue climbing along the cliffs (the trail to the right leads out to a

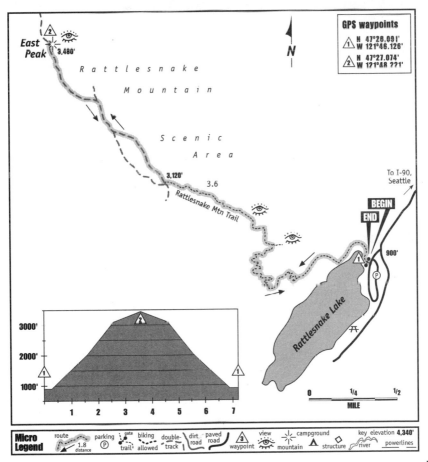

View from Rattlesnake Ledge

dramatic overlook). From here, say goodbye to the wide trail and lines of hikers. Stay on the main trail, as several lesser trails spur off to the right to promontory viewpoints. The Cedar River Watershed lies to the left, the trail acting as the northern boundary.

The way alternates between thick forest and open salal-covered slopes. After passing through an obviously man-made terraced clearing, **2.5 miles**, ascend to an old road. Turn right, following the trail signs. Stay on the main road as you climb. When the road divides at **3.0 miles**, bear left. At **3.5 miles**, look for the antenna tower on the right and take the first trail up, reaching the East Peak at **3.6 miles**.

Gazetteer

Nearby camping: Denny Creek Campground
Nearest food, drink, services: North Bend

NOTES:

_____

_____

_____

_____

3/5/05

Hike 11 ⛰ ⛰
TWIN FALLS ✓

Distance	**4.2-mile out and back**
Elevation	Low point: 620 ft., high point: 1,340 ft., **cumulative gain: 1,300 ft.**
Hike Time	2 to 4 hours, day hike
Travel	35 miles from Seattle
Season	Year round
Map	Green Trails: *Mount Si NRCA 206S*
Restrictions	State Parks vehicle fee, day use only, dogs on leash
More Info	Washington State Parks, 360-902-8844, www.parks.wa.gov

Trail Notes

Twin Falls, a spectacular set of waterfalls at Olallie State Park, is one of the gems close to Seattle. Wide and well-traveled, the trail spins through a lovely old-growth forest along the South Fork of the Snoqualmie River before climbing several steep pitches. The payoff is good, though: rocky canyons and shooting water.

Driving Directions

From Seattle, take Interstate 90 to Exit 34. At the end of the interstate ramp, zero out your odometer and turn right on 468th Avenue S.E. At 0.6 mile, turn left on S.E. 159th Street. The road ends at the trailhead parking area at 1.2 miles.

The Hike

From the parking area, Twin Falls Trail heads south along the South Fork of the Snoqualmie River. The river is wide here, and it's tempting to sit on the bank and gaze out at the riffles until long after it's time to return to the trailhead. And while the views on this hike get more spectacular, they don't get any more pleasant.

At **0.5 mile**, the trail bends to the east, leaving the river's edge, and switchbacks up a steep bank. It's a healthy climb through a dark forest, but the trail's tread is smooth. Cross over the ridge at **0.7 mile**. The trail descends for a short distance, winds upward again, then levels. Reach a fork at **0.9 mile**. The trail on the right stairsteps down about 200 yards to a dramatic wood platform perched high on the rocky canyon. It affords an awesome view of the lower falls. (I haven't counted this spur trail in the mileage, but I highly recommend it.) To continue up toward

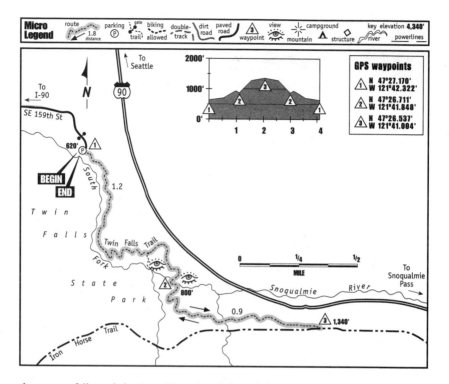

the upper falls and the Iron Horse Trail, bear left at the fork.

At **1.2 miles**, arrive at a bridge over the river. From here you can see the smaller upper falls, and you can watch the river vanish over the edge of the lower falls. It's a lovely spot, although it can be crowded on weekends. (This is a fine turnaround point. The rest of the way is less traveled but also much less scenic.) From the bridge, the trail climbs south up the lower steep slopes of Mount Washington, away from the river. At **1.4 miles**, the trail heads east again, traversing the bank and paralleling the Iron Horse rail-trail. At **2.1 miles**, reach the rail-trail. You can either turn right or left on this wide gravel trail and explore, or you can turn around and head back to the trailhead, **4.2 miles**.

Gazetteer

Nearby camping: Denny Creek Campground
Nearest food, drink, services: North Bend

NOTES:

Hike 12 ⛰ ⛰ ⛰
LITTLE MOUNT SI

Distance	5-mile out and back
Elevation	Low point: 470 ft., high point: 1,580 ft., **cumulative gain: 1,250 ft.**
Hike Time	2 to 4 hours, day hike
Travel	33 miles from Seattle
Season	Year round
Map	Green Trails: Mount Si NRCA 206S
Restrictions	Day use only, dogs on leash
More Info	Washington State Department of Natural Resources, South Puget Sound Region, 360-825-1631, www.wa.gov/dnr/

Trail Notes

This is a nice, year-round hike, but we have to discuss parking, an unfortunate discussion for a hiking book. The small dirt parking area holds about 15 vehicles. If it's full, and on Saturdays and Sundays year round it usually fills, you can try parking on the far side of the Middle Fork bridge, which is not a great choice because there's no walkway across the bridge. Just don't park closer to the trailhead on 434th Avenue S.E., because your car may be towed while you enjoy the pleasant forests of Little Si. If you continue past the small trailhead at 434th Avenue S.E., you'll find another parking area for Little Si on the left. Since this is a very popular trail, it's doubly important to keep your pooch on a leash and to not cut any switchbacks. Parts of this route are quite steep, almost a scramble, but most people shouldn't have trouble.

Driving Directions

From Seattle, take Interstate 90 to Exit 31. At the end of the exit ramp, set your odometer to zero and turn left onto Bendigo Boulevard S. At 0.7 miles, turn right onto North Bend Way. At 2.0 miles, take a left onto S.E. Mount Si Road.

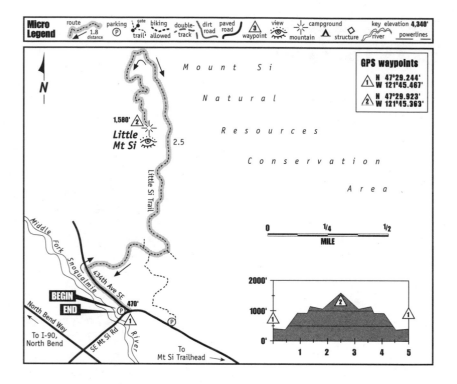

Cross the Middle Fork of the Snoqualmie River, then turn left on 434th Avenue S.E. at 2.4 miles. Immediately turn left again into the small dirt parking area tucked between Mount Si Road and 434th Avenue S.E. You can also continue on Mount Si Road for a short distance to find a second trailhead parking area for Little Si.

The Hike

From the parking area, walk away from Mount Si Road on 434th Avenue S.E., which is paved. It's a quiet road, but the lack of sidewalks demands careful walking. After about **0.3 mile**, time enough for a short dip and roll to the right, find Little Mount Si Trailhead on the right. The wide gravel trail cuts between houses, ascending through a corridor of thick salmonberry, accompanied by maple and red alder. This is one of the steeper sections of the trail.

At **0.5 mile**, the trail, still wide and graveled, levels. During the winter, when the alders haven't leafed out yet, you can see the summit of Little Si up to the left. Stay on the main trail, ignoring three lesser spurs on the right. The path descends slightly. Then at **0.7 miles**, cross over a small creek. From here, the trail narrows and climbs again, reaching into a coniferous forest of fir and cedar with a fern understory. The trail is rocky in places and root-strewn. Pass by a swale on the right populated by red alder.

A little farther on, pass a small and unexpected kiosk, then ignore several lesser trails on the left that lead to high rock cliffs, the east face of Little Si. On many days you'll see climbers dangling from ropes on these cliffs. Stay on the main trail. After another rise, with the base of the cliffs close on the right, reach a high point, **1.3 miles.** Traverse through a narrow, fern-filled valley— huge hemlock and cedar, large rock boulders, and nurse logs exposing brick-red viscera—that's shaped by Little Si on the left and Mount Si on the right. After a gradual descent through the narrow valley, the trail becomes more rugged as it climbs steeply up the north spine of Little Si.

Fern and moss give way to a drier understory of salal and Oregon grape and finally pockets of manzanita surrounded by wirey pine as the trail scrambles upward, over roots, around hanging trees, and up rocky trellises. In the end, the summit—a USGS marker names the spot Small Si— *Just south of Little Si* comes quickly, and the views open up unexpectedly, **2.5 miles.** Turn around and retrace your steps to complete the hike, **5.0 miles.**

Gazetteer

Nearby camping: Denny Creek Campground
Nearest food, drink, services: North Bend

NOTES:

Hike 13 ⛰ ⛰ ⛰
MOUNT SI

Distance	8-mile out and back
Elevation	Low point: 700 ft., high point: 3,900 ft., **cumulative gain: 3,300 ft.**
Hike Time	2 to 4 hours, day hike
Travel	36 miles from Seattle
Season	May through October
Map	Green Trails: *Mount Si NRCA 206S*
Restrictions	Day use only, dogs on leash
More Info	Washington State Department of Natural Resources, South Puget Sound Region, 360-825-1631, www.wa.gov/dnr/

Mount Si's haystack in late fall

Trail Notes

This is the Space Needle of Seattle-area hikes. Seattleites become hikers because of Mount Si, and that's a good thing. You don't have to buy a ticket, but of course you don't get the elevator ride either. Mount Si is almost always crowded, so don't plan for solitude. It even has three dirt parking lots to hold all of the weekend cars. But it's an area classic (and the book's namesake) because it's close, it's tough, and it's scenic—if you can make it to the top.

Driving Directions

From Seattle, take Interstate 90 eastbound to Exit 31. At the end of the exit ramp, set your odometer to zero and turn left onto Bendigo Boulevard S. At 0.7 miles, turn right onto North Bend Way. At 2.0 miles, take a left onto S.E. Mount Si Road, and at 4.7 miles, turn left into the huge parking area for the Mount Si Trailhead.

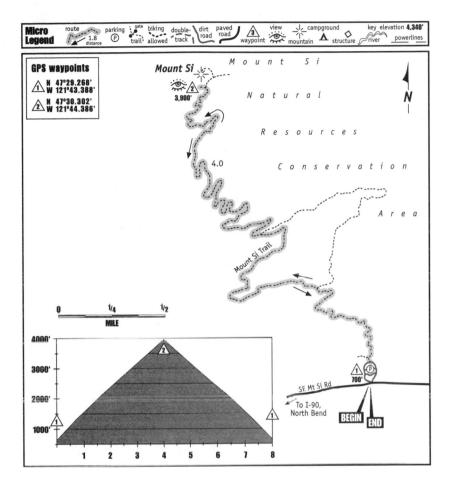

The Hike

From the parking area, follow the signs past the picnic area to Mount Si Trail. For a trail that gets so much attention and so much use, it's surprisingly rough, with rocks and large roots covering much of the first few miles. With an elevation gain of 800 feet per mile, it's also steep. At the fork, **0.1 mile**, bear right. The trail immediately starts the ascent, switchbacking up the south slope of Mount Si through a dark forest.

At **1.8 miles**, reach Snag Flats, which represents a short break in the climb. A boardwalk and sign here point out a 350-year-old Douglas fir that survived the catastrophic 1910 Mount Si fire. Alas, the flats are really more of a short ledge

Mount Si Trail in fog

than a true rest, and the trail heads relentlessly up again. As the trail picks and claws its way up the mountain, trail signs note the elevation and mileage every half mile.

At **3.8 miles**, the forest thins and breaks, and the trail emerges below a large rockfall. At **4.0 miles**, gain the high southern shoulder of the mountain—**Oof!**—just below the rock-cap summit known as the Haystack. The climb up the Haystack is a tricky scramble and can be treacherous in adverse conditions. Instead, eat your lunch in among the large rocks and soak in the views of the South Fork of the Snoqualmie River valley. Be sure to leave enough time to descend the mountain, as the roots, rocks, and steep descent, particularly the last few miles, make the down-hiking hard.

Gazetteer

Nearby camping: Denny Creek Campground
Nearest food, drink, services: North Bend

NOTES:

Hike 14 ▲ ▲ ▲

MIDDLE FORK OF THE SNOQUALMIE RIVER

Distance	12.2-mile out and back
Elevation	Low point: 1,030 ft., high point: 1,400 ft., **cumulative gain: 600 ft.**
Hike Time	4 to 7 hours, day hike
Travel	46 miles from Seattle
Season	April through October
Maps	Green Trails: *Mount Si 174, Skykomish 175*
Restrictions	NW Forest Pass
More Info	Mt. Baker-Snoqualmie National Forest, Snoqualmie District (North Bend), 425-888-1421, www.fs.fed.us/r6/mbs/

Trail Notes

The lovely river and old-growth forest are the highlights here. Rugged and majestic, surrounded by rock and wilderness, the Middle Fork of the Snoqualmie River valley is one of those most beautiful places. The hike isn't difficult, and the turnaround at the Dingford bridge is arbitrary, so you may want to leave it to your stomach and your legs and your forest aesthetic to decide when to have lunch and head back. The Forest Service has rebuilt much of the first few miles, eliminating the gooey clay bogs ready to snatch unsuspecting sneakers. Note: Bicycles will likely be allowed on the trail during the summer and early fall on an every-other-day basis.

Driving Directions

From Seattle, take Interstate 90 eastbound to Exit 34. At the end of the exit ramp, set your odometer to zero and turn left. At 0.4 mile, turn right onto S.E. Middle Fork Road. Reach a fork, 1.4 miles, and bear right. At 3 miles, the road becomes dirt. At 12.4 miles, find the large dirt parking area on the right.

The Middle Fork

The Hike

From the parking area, the trail cuts through the woods to a suspension bridge over the Middle Fork of the Snoqualmie River. Cross the bridge, turn left, and

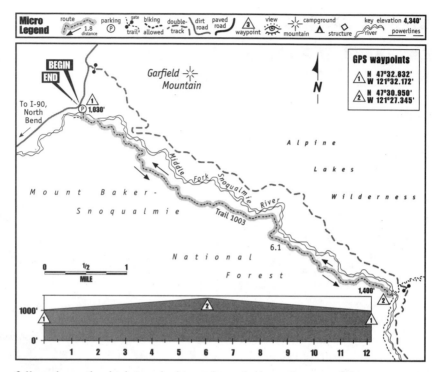

follow the trail, which is etched into the rock above the powerful current.

At **0.2 mile**, the trail eases away from the river into the lush forest that populates the bottom of the valley. It's a mixed forest of alder and fir, and dark due to the sheer mountainside that rises up on the right. The trail follows the rolls and swells of the bench between river and steep mountainside, sometimes staying close to the water, other times snugging up against the base of the cliffs. As you gently ascend, you'll cross numerous bridges and wood walkways that span tributaries and wetlands. At **6.0 miles**, reach a fork and bear left. At **6.1 miles**, reach another bridge over the river about one quarter-mile below the Dingford Creek Trailhead.

Gazetteer

Nearby camping: Tinkham Campground
Nearest food, drink, services: North Bend

NOTES:

Hike 15 ▲ ▲ ▲ ▲

HESTER LAKE

Distance	**11-mile out and back**
Elevation	Low point: 1,500 ft., high point: 3,900 ft., **cumulative gain: 2,950 ft.**
Hike Time	4 to 7 hours, day hike or overnight
Travel	53 miles from Seattle
Season	July through October
Map	Green Trails: *Skykomish 175*
Restrictions	NW Forest Pass, dogs on leash, no fires, max group 12
More Info	Mt. Baker-Snoqualmie National Forest, Snoqualmie District (North Bend), 425-888-1421, www.fs.fed.us/r6/mbs/

Trail Notes

The trail to Hester Lake is much more difficult than its sister trail to Myrtle Lake (see Hike 16). After the fork that separates the two routes, the trail to Hester turns boggy and faint and requires a number of stream fords. Above, as you climb toward the lake, there's a short scramble up a lattice of roots. Given these hiking challenges, the trail to Hester is less travelled than the trail to Myrtle. But Hester Lake is bigger and wilder than Myrtle Lake, with steep forested hillsides surrounding it, and it's worth the extra effort. Note that Forest Road 56 may be gated six miles before the trailhead, so call ahead to check on the status.

Driving Directions

From Seattle, take Interstate 90 eastbound to Exit 34. At the end of the exit ramp, set your odometer to zero and turn left. At 0.4 mile, turn right onto S.E. Middle Fork Road. At 1.4 miles, reach a fork and bear right. The road becomes dirt at 3.0 miles. Continue to 12.5 miles and pass the lower parking area for the Middle Fork Trail on the right. At 12.9 miles, turn right on Forest Road 56. From here to the trailhead, the road is quite rough and slow going. At 19 miles, reach the parking area for Dingford Creek Trailhead on the right.

First glimpse of Hester Lake

63

The Hike

Dingford Creek Trail 1005 begins on the opposite side of the road from the parking area. The trail starts out steep, rocky, and root-strewn. It switchbacks up the sometimes wet hillside, among vine maple, salal, fern, and devil's club. Around **1.0 mile**, enter the Alpine Lakes Wilderness. At **1.2 miles**, cross the creek that tumbles down from Pumpkinseed Lake. This signals the end of the difficult climbing. From here, the trail runs smoother on pine needle and duff—for a while.

The trail traverses through a sweet old-growth forest just north of the rush of Dingford Creek. At **3.0 miles**, reach a fork and bear right, following the sign toward Hester Lake. From the fork, the trail descends gradually southward to Dingford Creek, becoming fainter and brushier as it goes. At **3.4 miles**, ford the

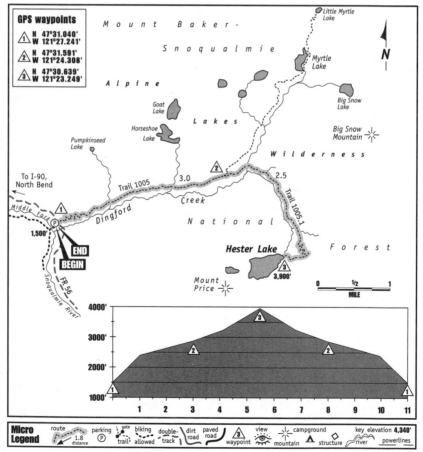

Hester Lake and Mount Price

creek. The trail is boggy and root-strewn. You'll need to ford several more creeks, and just as the trail seems to have disappeared altogether, a sign points the way to Hester Lake.

The trail, still wet and hard to follow, parallels the stream that drains from the lake. Near the head of the valley, the way gets steep again, and there's a short scramble. **Oof!** Soon after, though, the trail traverses west. Pass a pothole on the left, then quickly the lake comes into view. Reach the eastern tip at **5.5 miles**. Forested slopes on the west end of the lake rise toward Mount Price.

Gazetteer

Nearby camping: Tinkham Campground
Nearest food, drink, services: North Bend

NOTES:

_____

_____

_____

_____

Hike 16 ▲ ▲ ▲ ▲

MYRTLE LAKE

Distance	11-mile out and back
Elevation	Low point: 1,500 ft., high point: 3,780 ft., **cumulative gain: 2,800 ft.**
Hike Time	4 to 6 hours, day hike or overnight
Travel	53 miles from Seattle
Season	July through October
Map	Green Trails: *Skykomish 175*
Restrictions	NW Forest Pass, dogs on leash, max group 12
More Info	Mt. Baker-Snoqualmie National Forest, Snoqualmie District (North Bend), 425-888-1421, www.fs.fed.us/r6/mbs/

Trail Notes

This is a moderately popular trail on summer weekends. However, the Forest Service may gate the road six miles from the trailhead, upping the trail's solitude quotient by making it more difficult to get there. Even now Forest Road 56 is quite rough. How about a bike and hike opportunity? The bottom line: Call ahead to check on the status. The first mile of this trail is difficult, rocky and root-strewn, and demands an agile hiker. After that, though, the grade mellows, the trail smoothes, and you'll enjoy the sublime Alpine Lakes Wilderness forest.

Driving Directions

From Seattle, take Interstate 90 eastbound to Exit 34. At the end of the exit ramp, set your odometer to zero and turn left. At 0.4 mile, turn right onto S.E. Middle Fork Road. At 1.4 miles, reach a fork and bear right. The road becomes dirt at 3.0 miles. Continue to 12.5 miles and pass the lower parking area for the Middle Fork Trail on the right. At 12.9 miles, turn right on Forest Road 56. The road is quite rough from here. At 19 miles, reach the parking area for Dingford Creek Trailhead on the right.

The Hike

Dingford Creek Trail 1005 begins on the opposite side of the road from the parking area. The trail is steep, quite rocky, and often wet right from the start, as it switchbacks up the hillside. Beneath the Douglas fir and hemlock, an understory of vine maple, salal, Oregon grape, and fern flourishes. At about **1.0 mile**, enter the Alpine Lakes Wilderness. Afterward, the trail smoothes out—more duff, less rocks—and the uphill grade is more gradual. At **1.2 miles**, cross the creek that tumbles down from Pumpkinseed Lake. This signals the end of the difficult climbing.

But the ascent continues through old growth, as devil's club reach across the forest amid the crash and rush of Dingford Creek. At **3.0 miles**, reach a fork and

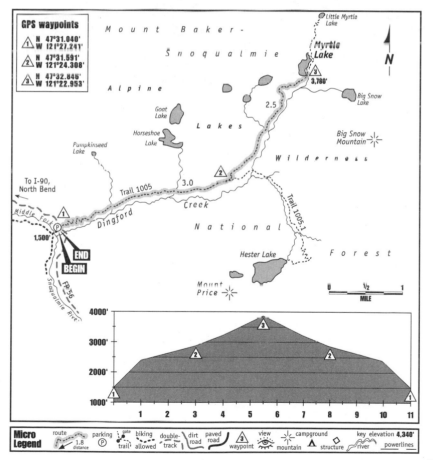

Myrtle Lake

bear left, following the sign to Myrtle Lake. After crossing a creek, gradually climb into the mountain hemlock zone, with occasional Alaska cedar. The tread can be quite muddy at times, and the footing occasionally awkward. At **5.5 miles**, reach Myrtle Lake. You'll find a nice campsite immediately across the outlet stream and a great view of Big Snow Mountain up to the right.

Gazetteer

Nearby camping: Tinkham Campground
Nearest food, drink, services: North Bend

NOTES:

_____

_____

_____

_____

Hike 17 ⛰ ⛰ ⛰ ⛰ ⛰

NORDRUM LAKE

Distance	16.6-mile out and back
Elevation	Low point: 1,160 ft., high point: 3,780 ft., **cumulative gain: 3,500 ft.**
Hike Time	7 to 12 hours, day hike or overnight
Travel	47 miles from Seattle
Season	July through October
Maps	Green Trails: *Mount Si 174, Skykomish 175*
Restrictions	NW Forest Pass, dogs on leash, max group 12
More Info	Mt. Baker-Snoqualmie National Forest, Snoqualmie District (North Bend), 425-888-1421, www.fs.fed.us/r6/mbs/

Trail Notes

This is one of the very few 5-peak hikes. Not only is it one of the longer hikes in this volume, but it's also difficult hiking (it's not regularly maintained) and easy to get lost. After a tricky ford of the Taylor River, you'll climb and scramble up roots, past ferns, and through myriad spider webs spun to turn back the most determined hiker. This section from the river to the lake can be hard to follow, so make sure to drop your bread crumbs as you go. But Nordrum's a beautiful lake, and you won't regret the trip after you get back and have a good story to tell.

Driving Directions

From Seattle, take Interstate 90 eastbound to Exit 34. At the end of the exit ramp, set your odometer to zero and turn left. At 0.4 mile, turn right onto S.E. Middle Fork Road. At 1.4 miles, reach a fork and bear right. The road becomes dirt at 3.0 miles. Continue to 12.5 miles and pass the lower parking area for the Middle Fork Trail on the right. At 12.9 miles, reach a fork and bear left to a gate at 13.4 miles. Park here alongside the road.

The Hike

Walk around the gate, heading north on the gravelly road, and immediately cross the Taylor River. When the road forks at **0.4 miles**, take the lesser fork to the right. **Whoa!** This is an easy turn to miss. This is the old Taylor River Road, which is now part trail, part road, and part rock garden. The trail gains elevation slowly, paralleling the river.

Pass over Martin Creek on an old wooden bridge at **2.8 miles**. Just beyond, cross over a small landslide. At **4.8 miles**, reach the paved bridge over Otter Creek. Above, Otter Falls sheets over large rocks. From here, the trail is sometimes brushy. At **5.7 miles**, the wide trail descends slightly. Note that you've gained only 600 feet to this point. At **5.8 miles**, the way divides, with a dirt trail that climbs toward Snoqualmie Lake on the left and a wide, gravelly trail that descends (for now) on its way toward Nordrum Lake on the right. Take the right fork and walk down to its rendezvous with Taylor River.

At **5.9 miles**, you'll need to ford Taylor River—both channels. **Whoa!** This can be treacherous in high water, and it makes sense to spend some time looking for a safe route across. Hike a short distance and then cross over the second channel. Some downed trees span the river here. Almost immediately after crossing the

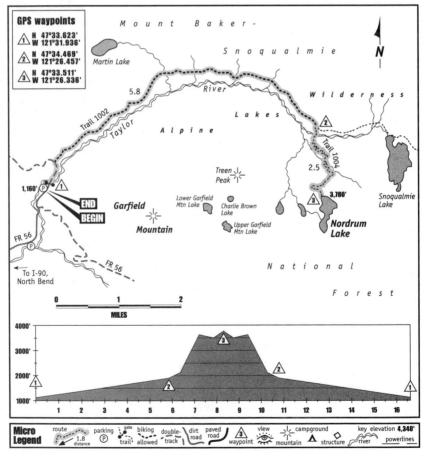

Early season at Nordrum Lake

river, you enter the Alpine Lakes Wilderness, where you'll meander past gigantic cedar and hemlock. But at **6.2 miles**, the trail, which is faint and often muddy, turns incredibly steep, and the next two miles resemble, as much as any section of trail in this book, an out-and-out bushwhack.

Root gardens, wet with mud and running water and lined with deer fern and Canadian dogwood, form long sections of the trail and make the footing awkward and, at times, dangerous. As the switchbacks scramble up the east side of a small creek, you'll see occasional views to the west of Treen Peak. At **6.7 miles**, cross to the west side of the creek over a smooth rock waterfall. **Whoa!** Be careful on this crossing. From here, the trail is faint, brushy, and easily lost as it zigzags up along the west side of the creek.

At **7.4 miles**, the trail bears to the right and traverses west, climbing still, but at a less hectic rate. The traverse affords views of the high ridges and peaks across the Taylor River valley. At one point the trail drops and crosses a boulder field, then bears to the left and heads straight up a steep draw. At **8.1 miles**, cross through a saddle. **Oof!** The strenuous climb is over. The forest is open here, sporting hemlock and Alaska cedar. Just over the saddle, you'll see Nordrum Lake below. The trail drops to the lake at **8.3 miles**. Make sure to save some energy and daylight for the difficult down-hiking back to the car.

Gazetteer
Nearby camping: Tinkham Campground
Nearest food, drink, services: North Bend

NOTES:

Hike 18 ⛰ ⛰ ⛰ ⛰

SNOQUALMIE LAKE

Distance	15-mile out and back
Elevation	Low point: 1,160 ft., high point: 3,160 ft., **cumulative gain: 2,300 ft.**
Hike Time	5 to 10 hours, day hike or overnight
Travel	47 miles from Seattle
Season	June through October
Maps	Green Trails: *Mount Si 174, Skykomish 175*
Restrictions	NW Forest Pass, dogs on leash, max group 12
More Info	Mt. Baker-Snoqualmie National Forest, Snoqualmie District (North Bend), 425-888-1421, www.fs.fed.us/r6/mbs/

Trail Notes

In contrast to its evil twin, Nordrum Lake (see Hike 17), it's a cakewalk to Snoqualmie Lake. This route opens up a little earlier than most, usually by sometime in June. Since the Taylor River Trail, the first 5.8 miles of the route, is open to mountain bikes, this represents a possible bike and hike opportunity—a great way to beat the crowds.

Driving Directions

From Seattle, take Interstate 90 eastbound to Exit 34. At the end of the exit ramp, set your odometer to zero and turn left. At 0.4 mile, turn right onto S.E. Middle Fork Road. At 1.4 miles, reach a fork and bear right. The road becomes dirt, 3.0 miles, and at 12.5 miles, passes the lower parking area for the Middle Fork Trail on the right. At 12.9 miles, reach a fork and bear left. At 13.4 miles, reach a gate and park alongside the road.

Otter Falls

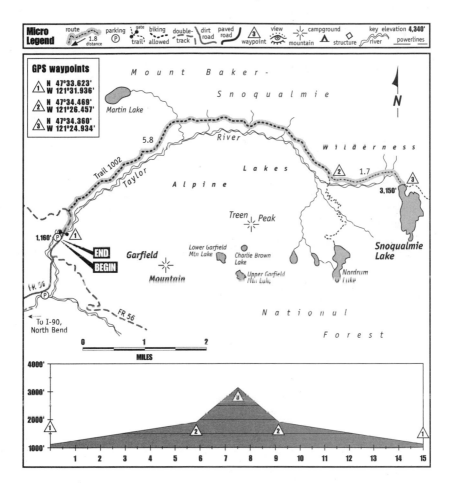

GPS waypoints

⚠1 N 47°33.623' W 121°31.936'

⚠2 N 47°34.469' W 121°26.457'

⚠3 N 47°34.360' W 121°24.934'

The Hike

Walk around the gate, heading north on the decommissioned road, and immediately cross the Taylor River. The gravelly road forks at **0.4 miles**—take the lesser fork to the right. **Whoa!** This is an easy turn to miss. This is the old Taylor River Road, which is now part trail, part road, and part rock garden.

Pass over Martin Creek on an old wooden bridge at **2.8 miles**. Just beyond, cross over a small landslide. At **4.8 miles**, reach the paved bridge over Otter Creek. Above, Otter Falls sheets over large rocks. From here, the trail is sometimes brushy. At **5.7 miles**, the way descends slightly. Note that you've only gained 600 feet to this point. Reach a fork at **5.8 miles** and bear left, climbing toward Snoqualmie Lake.

Almost immediately after the fork, you'll pass into the Alpine Lakes Wilderness. The trail ascends sharply, continuing to parallel Taylor River through a rich old-growth forest. At **7.0 miles**, the trail crosses several creeks, then veers to the right. At **7.5 miles**, reach the northern tip of Snoqualmie Lake. The trail continues on from here, climbing east to Deer Lake, Bear Lake, and Lake Dorothy (see Hike 38).

Gazetteer

Nearby camping: Tinkham Campground
Nearest food, drink, services: North Bend

NOTES:

_____

_____

_____

_____

Hike 19 ⛰ ⛰ ⛰ ⛰

McCLELLAN BUTTE

Distance	8.8-mile out and back
Elevation	Low point: 1,500 ft., high point: 5,160 ft., **cumulative gain: 3,800 ft.**
Hike Time	3 to 5 hours, day hike
Travel	43 miles from Seattle
Season	July through October
Map	Green Trails: *Bandera 206*
Restrictions	NW Forest Pass
More Info	Mt. Baker-Snoqualmie National Forest, Snoqualmie District (North Bend), 425-888-1421, www.fs.fed.us/r6/mbs/

Trail Notes

Here's a peak bagger's hike if there ever was one. McClellan Butte is a southern sister to Mount Si in a way, but with a lot less people. It's also a less interesting hike until you gain the high ridge. Note: Bikes are allowed the first mile.

Driving Directions

From Seattle, drive east on Interstate 90. Take Exit 42 to Tinkham Road. At the end of the exit ramp, set your odometer to zero and turn right. At 0.3 mile, turn right on Forest Road 5500-101 toward McClellan Butte Trailhead. Reach the trailhead at 0.5 mile.

The Hike

McClellan Butte Trail 1015 noodles through a sparse forest. At **0.2 mile**, cross under a set of power lines and enter a thick, second-growth forest, climbing now. The trail crosses an overgrown logging road. Almost immediately, **0.4 mile**, reach the Iron Horse Trail, a rail-trail, and turn right. The rail-trail is wide and flat. At **0.8 mile**, McClellan Butte Trail starts up again on the left. Take it. From here, the trail climbs steeply, again through a dark forest devoid of undergrowth. The route is dark, shadowing Alice Creek, and if you're alone it's easy to won-

Foxglove in the forest

75

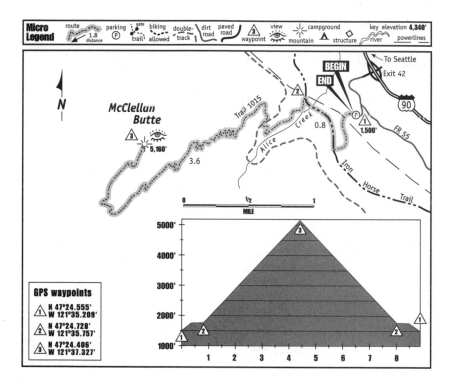

der if you're travelling through caverns to meet up with Gollum.

At **1.2 miles**, cross a gravel road. The incline of the trail gradually tilts upward, and before too long you are frantically switchbacking up the eastern flank of the butte. At about the **3.0-mile** mark, the trail stops switchbacking but continues ascending. The trail cuts a steep uphill traverse to the southern backside of the butte where it mounts a ridge. At **3.8 miles**, the trail meets up with the ridgeline, which is open and meadowed. **Oof!** After a short scramble, reach the top of the butte, at **4.4 miles**.

Gazetteer

Nearby camping: Tinkham Campground

Nearest food, drink, services: Snoqualmie Pass

NOTES:

Hike 20  ▲ ▲ ▲

ANNETTE LAKE

Distance	**7-mile out and back**
Elevation	Low point: 1,900 ft., high point: 3,630 ft., **cumulative gain: 1,900 ft.**
Hike Time	3 to 5 hours, day hike
Travel	48 miles from Seattle
Season	July through October
Map	Green Trails: *Snoqualmie Pass 207*
Restrictions	NW Forest Pass
More Info	Mt. Baker-Snoqualmie National Forest, Snoqualmie District (North Bend), 425-888-1421, www.fs.fed.us/r6/mbs/

Trail Notes

It's a healthy climb up to Annette Lake, but not too intense, and a mountain lake close to Seattle that's not too strenuous is always a draw. Thus and so, this is an extremely popular hike, and on summer weekends the large parking area often fills up. The trail is rocky and root-strewn in places, especially over the first mile, but mostly it's in good condition. Campsites are available at the lake, though overnight camping is not recommended due to the high impact of crowds on the fragile lake system. A short and beautiful interpretive trail also begins from the trailhead. Note: Bikes are allowed on the first mile of trail, to access the Iron Horse Trail.

Driving Directions

From Seattle, take Interstate 90 eastbound to Exit 47. At the end of the exit ramp, set your odometer to zero and turn right. At 0.1 mile, reach a T and turn left toward Annette Lake Trail. At 0.5 mile, turn right into the large, paved Annette Lake Trail parking area.

Log bridge toward Annette Lake

The Hike

Head to the kiosk at the east end of the parking area. An interpretive trail begins on the left. Instead, bear right and walk around a gate that's signed Road Closed. Immediately after the gate, turn left on Annette Lake Trail 1019. Your first few steps begin the steady climb you'll maintain for much of the way to the lake. The trail, wide but quite rough with a staircase of imbedded rocks and large roots, switchbacks up through a dark second-growth forest.

At **0.2 mile**, cross over Humpback Creek, an energetic tumble of water that's fed by Annette Lake and the runoff from Humpback Mountain and Silver Peak. At **0.4 mile**, the trail crosses an old roadbed. At **0.7 mile**, reach the Iron Horse Trail, a wide, gravel rail-trail. Cross the Iron Horse and continue up the Annette

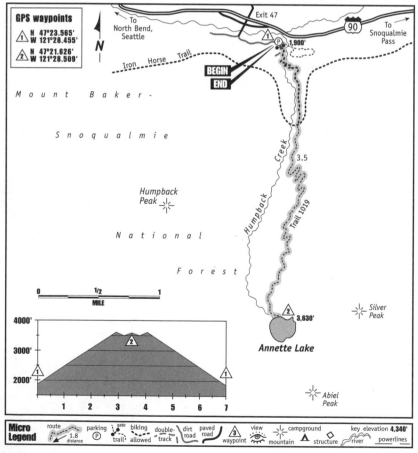

Humphack Creek

Lake Trail. From here, the trail continues ascending at a steady rate, but the tread is smoother, with fewer rocks and roots.

Several short sections of the trail are quite steep. But around the **2.5-mile** point, the way levels and begins traversing across the steep western slope of Silver Peak. The traverse rolls for the next mile, switchbacking up and then dropping down, in and out of tiny Silver Peak stream cuts and across several rocky slopes that provide modest territorial views. At **3.5 miles**, reach the lake, which is surrounded by high forested walls that stretch up to rocky ridges.

Gazetteer

Nearby camping: Tinkham Campground
Nearest food, drink, services: North Bend, Snoqualmie Pass

NOTES:

_____

_____

_____

_____

Hike 21 ⛰️⛰️

TALAPUS LAKE

Distance	**4.4-mile out and back** (5.8-mile option)
Elevation	Low point: 2,600 ft., high point: 3,340 ft., **cumulative gain: 900 ft.**
Hike Time	2 to 3 hours, day hike
Travel	48 miles from Seattle
Season	July through October
Map	Green Trails: *Bandera 206*
Restrictions	NW Forest Pass, dogs on leash, no fires, max group 12
More Info	Mt. Baker-Snoqualmie National Forest, Snoqualmie District (North Bend), 425-888-1421, www.fs.fed.us/r6/mbs/

Trail Notes

Talapus is a Chinook word for coyote, but given all the people, I doubt you'll see a coyote here. It's a very short hike and incredibly busy; if you're going on a weekend and don't arrive early, you might have to park a mile or more from the start of the trail. None the less, it's a great hike for kids—short, but with an alpine feel. Talapus Lake is not recommended for camping.

Driving Directions

From Seattle, take Interstate 90 eastbound to Exit 45, about 13 miles east of North Bend. At the end of the exit ramp, set your odometer to zero and turn left to cross north under the interstate. At 0.5 mile, the road turns to dirt, and at 0.9 mile, it reaches a fork; turn right on Forest Road 9030. At 3.4 miles, reach the trailhead and park.

The Hike

The trail to Talapus Lake gets a lot of foot traffic. And you can tell. The tread starts out wide and compact as it switchbacks up the eastern shoulder of Bandera Mountain. The trail is shaded by big fir trees for the entire route. Roots make the footing tricky in places. At **1.2 miles**, the switchbacks close in on Talapus Creek, located down a tight draw to the east.

At **1.9 miles**, cross over the creek. Early in the season, the trail can be muddy here. At **2.2 miles**, the trail kisses Talapus Lake. Take any one of the lesser trails on the left to the lake.

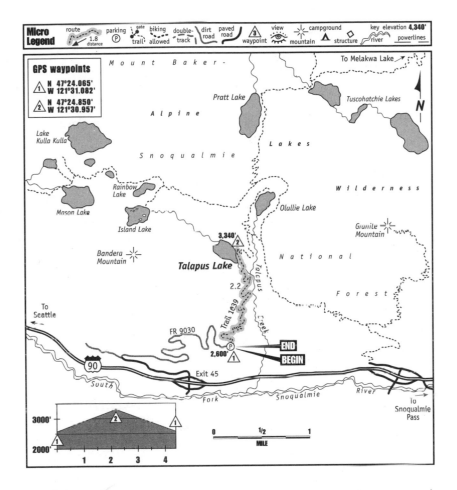

Option

From Talapus Lake, continue up the main trail. At 2.4 miles, reach a fork and bear left. After a short climb, reach the west shore of Olallie Lake, 2.9 miles.

Gazetteer

Nearby camping: Denny Creek Campground, Tinkham Campground
Nearest food, drink, services: Snoqualmie Pass

NOTES:

_____

_____

Hike 22 ⛰ ⛰ ⛰ ⛰
PRATT LAKE

Distance	11.4-mile out and back
Elevation	Low point: 1,880 ft., high point: 4,200 ft., **cumulative gain: 3,400 ft.**
Hike Time	4 to 7 hours, day hike or overnight
Travel	48 miles from Seattle
Season	July through October
Maps	Green Trails: *Snoqualmie Pass 207, Bandera 206*
Restrictions	NW Forest Pass, dogs on leash, no fires, max group 12
More Info	Mt. Baker-Snoqualmie National Forest, Snoqualmie District (North Bend), 425-888-1421, www.fs.fed.us/r6/mbs/

Trail Notes

This is the classic Cascade trail, a duff tread through a fir and hemlock forest, which opens up occasionally to afford views of mountain lakes. It's well maintained and nicely graded, though there may be times when you wish it would stop going up. Pratt Lake is surrounded by talus slopes, but there are a few camp spots at the north end of the lake.

Driving Directions

From Seattle, drive east on Interstate 90. Take Exit 47. At the end of the exit ramp, set your odometer to zero and turn left. After crossing over I-90, reach a T and turn left, following the sign toward Granite Mountain Lookout. At 0.5 mile reach the trailhead and park.

Olallie Lake and Mount Rainier from Pratt Lake Trail

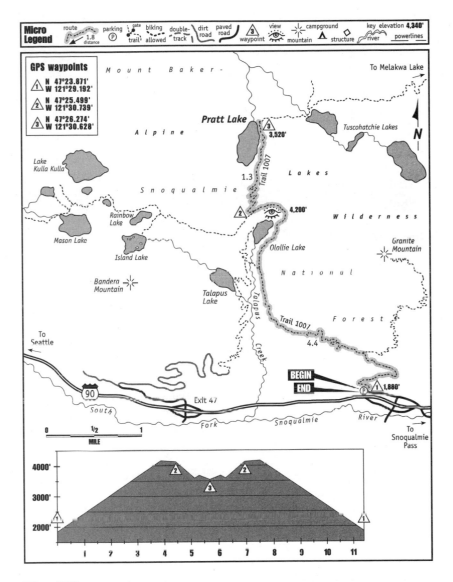

The Hike

From the trailhead, Pratt Lake Trail 1007, wide, well worn, and somewhat rocky, winds through a mixed forest. After gaining 800 feet, the trail forks at **1.2 miles**. Bear left at the fork, continuing up Trail 1007 toward Pratt Lake. This is a great section of trail—quiet, smooth, not too steep—through beautiful Northwest forest.

Pratt Lake

After swinging clockwise around the fat midsection of Granite Mountain, the trail divides at **3.1 miles**—bear right. The trail climbs to the north here, then winds around the upper end of Olallie Lake, on an open traverse, and you can see the lake several hundred feet below on the left. At **4.3 miles**, after you've traversed your way to an unexpected saddle, reach a fork and bear right.

The trail drops quickly into the Pratt Lake basin. Soon after the saddle, you can glimpse the lake through the trees, but the trail switchbacks here and there, then crosses a long talus field on the western slopes above the lake. At **5.7 miles**, the trail finally drops to the lake at its northern tip.

Gazetteer

Nearby camping: Denny Creek Campground, Tinkham Campground
Nearest food, drink, services: Snoqualmie Pass

NOTES:

_____

_____

_____

_____

Hike 23 ⛰️ ⛰️ ⛰️ ⛰️

GRANITE MOUNTAIN

Distance	8.6-mile out and back
Elevation	Low point: 1,800 ft., high point: 5,630 ft., **cumulative gain: 4,000 ft.**
Hike Time	3 to 6 hours, day hike
Travel	48 miles from Seattle
Season	June through October
Map	Green Trails: *Snoqualmie Pass 207*
Restrictions	NW Forest Pass, dogs on leash, no fires, max group 12
More Info	Mt. Baker-Snoqualmie National Forest, Snoqualmie District (North Bend), 425-888-1421, www.fs.fed.us/r6/mbs/

Trail Notes

Take a look at the elevation profile. It bests all but Mount Pugh (see Hike 59) in its relentless pyramid-ness. Need I say more? You won't find a lick of water on the climb either, and much of the trail runs out of tree cover, exposed to the sun. But the views are spectacular, and the trail generally opens up early.

Driving Directions

From Seattle, drive east on Interstate 90. Take Exit 47. At the end of the exit, zero your odometer and turn left. After crossing I-90, reach a T and turn left, heading toward Granite Mountain Lookout. At 0.5 mile, reach the trailhead.

The Hike

Right out of the blocks you'll begin a steady climb on Pratt Lake Trail 1007, wide and well pounded, as it winds through semi-dense forest. Enjoy it—the real climbing begins soon enough. After gaining 800 feet, the trail forks at **1.2 miles**—turn right on Granite Mountain Trail 1016.

Suddenly it's a different hike as the trail narrows, ratcheting up the lower south slope of Granite Mountain as steep as any Six Flags roller coaster, but thankfully away from the rush and buzz of the human carnival. Rocks and roots punctuate the climb. Short, ambitiously steep switchbacks cross back and forth between the mountain's fir and hemlock and steep open slopes.

After about **2.7 miles**, the trail swings east, offering a short traverse before mounting the ridge that spills southeast from the summit of the mountain. The

85

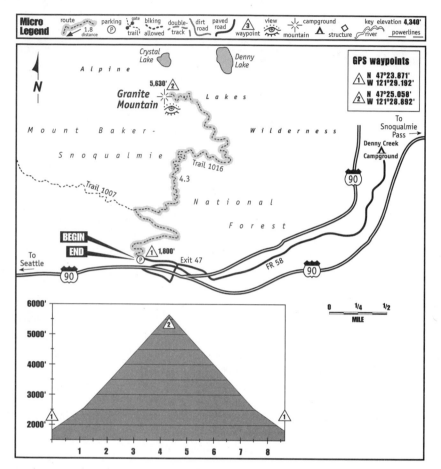

To Snoqualmie Pass →

trail, exposed to the sun, rocky and uneven, cuts through low brush and fields of wildflowers. At **3.1 miles**, the trail bends north again, climbing quickly. Cross into the Alpine Lakes Wilderness then follow the ridge northwest to the summit of Granite Mountain—**Oof!**—**4.3 miles**. The views from the fire lookout are worth the effort, with Mounts Rainier, Baker, Glacier, and Stuart highlighting.

Gazetteer

Nearby camping: Denny Creek Campground, Tinkham Campground
Nearest food, drink, services: Snoqualmie Pass

NOTES:

Hike 24 ⛰ ⛰ ⛰
MELAKWA LAKE ✓

Distance	**9.0-mile out and back**
Elevation	Low point: 2,300 ft., high point: 4,640 ft., **cumulative gain: 2,700 ft.**
Hike Time	4 to 7 hours, day hike or overnight
Travel	48 miles from Seattle
Season	July through October
Map	Green Trails: *Snoqualmie Pass 207*
Restrictions	NW Forest Pass, dogs on leash, no fires, max group 12
More Info	Mt. Baker-Snoqualmie National Forest, Snoqualmie District (North Bend), 425-888-1421, www.fs.fed.us/r6/mbs/

Trail Notes

This is one of those hikes that stereotypes trails in the Alpine Lakes Wilderness—an easily reached trailhead, a lovely high alpine lake at the base of steep talus slopes, and a bazillion people on sunny weekends. There's a cost when it's beautiful and relatively easy to get to. The other side of the coin: Melakwa is an Indian term for mosquito. And the route to the lake is rocky, root-strewn, steep, and exposed to the sun much of the way. But the snowfields that sweep down to kiss the lake from Chair and Bryant Peaks make the lake picturesque for sure. Just try going on a Wednesday to avoid the crowds. Being a longer hike and more of a climb than that to Snow, Talapus, or Olallie Lakes, the trail into Melakwa sees fewer people, and you can usually find a place to tuck in around the lake for lunch. If you continue on to Lower Tuscohatchie Lake, most of the day hikers disappear altogether.

Driving Directions

From Seattle, drive east on Interstate 90 past North Bend to Exit 47. Set your odometer to zero at the end of the exit ramp, and turn left. At 0.1 mile, reach a T and turn right. At 0.4 mile, reach a fork and bear left on Forest Road 58 toward Denny Creek Campground. At 2.7 miles, pass the campground on the left. At 3.0 miles, turn left on FR 5830 toward the Melakwa Lake Trailhead. Reach the trailhead at 3.2 miles and park.

The Hike

Follow Denny Creek Trail 1014, wide and smooth, through a rich cedar and fir forest, along a carefully crafted series of boardwalks, turnpikes, and bridges that protect the tread from hundreds of weekend boots. Cross over Denny Creek, then at **0.3 mile**, pass under the westbound span of I 90, which is supported by huge square pillars that look like giant petrified trees. From here, the trail gently climbs the north slope of Denny Creek.

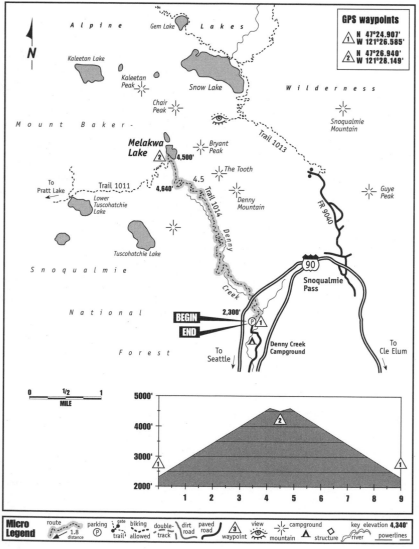

Melakwa Lake and Chair Peak

At **0.7 mile**, pass into the Alpine Lakes Wilderness. At **1.1 miles**, cross a bridge over Denny Creek at a wide granite slab called the Water Slide, a popular resting and play spot. A little farther, climb out of the cool of the big trees and begin a series of short and long switchbacks and traverses up a rocky trail, exposed to the sun much of the way. Denny Creek is on the right now, down a deep gorge. There's a great view of Keewulee Falls around the **1.9-mile** mark, and when it's sunny a rainbow persists on the falls all day.

The trail crosses Denny Creek again then traverses a couple of scree slopes. As you close in on Hemlock Pass, the grade is even but relentless, and the lack of shade can make it a sweat-fest. At **4.1 miles**, you gain the pass, the route's high point. Traverse north here, descending slightly along a sometimes-muddy, root-strewn tread. At **4.4 miles**, reach a fork and bear right toward Melakwa Lake (left to Tuscohatchie Lake). Melakwa Lake sits just over the rise, at **4.5 miles**, tucked beneath Bryant and Chair Peaks. Snowfields feed the lake well into August and year round on big snow years.

Gazetteer
Nearby camping: Denny Creek Campground, Tinkham
Nearest food, drink, services: Snoqualmie Pass

NOTES:

Hike 25 ⛰ ⛰ ⛰

SNOW LAKE

Distance	**6-mile out and back** (10-mile option)
Elevation	Low point: 3,150 ft., high point: 4,440 ft., **cumulative gain: 1,800 ft.**
Hike Time	2 to 5 hours, day hike or overnight
Travel	53 miles from Seattle
Season	July through October
Map	Green Trails: *Snoqualmie Pass 207*
Restrictions	NW Forest Pass, dogs on leash, no fires, max group 12
More Info	Mt. Baker-Snoqualmie National Forest, Snoqualmie District (North Bend), 425-888-1421, www.fs.fed.us/r6/mbs/

Trail Notes

Perhaps the most popular hike in the Alpine Lakes Wilderness, the trail to Snow Lake climbs through old-growth forests in sight of a dramatic trio of rocky summits—Denny Mountain and Bryant and Chair Peaks. Wildflowers and mountain grasses dress up the slanted meadows and boulder fields. At the head of the valley, the trail climbs to a saddle to reveal a view of the lake from above that is synonymous with the Alpine Lakes. It's beautiful, but there are crowds to contend with, so don't expect solitude. Camping is allowed at Snow Lake (in designated spots only), but Gem Lake and Wildcat Lakes beyond are better choices—for peace and quiet. Note: Some camp and picnic spots are closed for restoration.

Driving Directions

From Seattle, drive east on Interstate 90 to Snoqualmie Pass. Take Exit 52. At the end of the exit ramp, set your odometer to zero and turn left. At 0.1 mile, bear left. Almost immediately, bear right onto Forest Road 9040, following the signs toward Alpental Ski Area. Stay on the main road. At 1.3 miles, pass a gravel parking area on the left. At 1.4 miles, find a very large dirt parking area on the left.

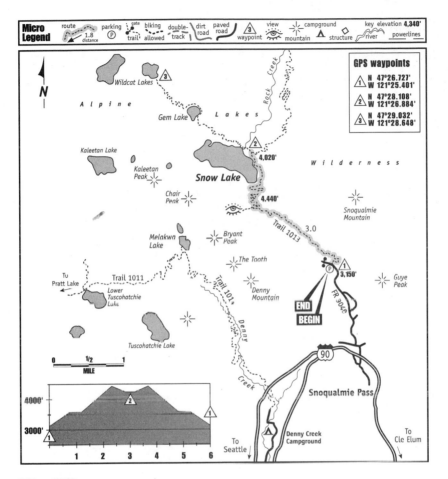

The Hike

Snow Lake Trail 1013 begins on the opposite side of FR 9040 from the large parking area. The trail immediately starts climbing away from the road. After a few switchbacks, the trail bears to the left and traverses up the valley, heading northwest parallel to the South Fork of the Snoqualmie River. It's forested, but you'll cross several open boulder fields along the way.

At **1.5 miles**, reach a fork and turn right. The trail, now rocky and exposed, switchbacks up a steep slope toward a saddle on the ridge that connects Chair Peak to the west and Snoqualmie Mountain off to the east. At **2.3 miles**, gain the saddle, which is shaded by big trees. It's here that you'll enter the Alpine Lakes Wilderness. Just beyond, you'll get the best view of Snow Lake, located 500 feet below to the north.

91

Snow Lake

The trail is more shaded as it drops toward the lake, switchbacking and weaving past granite boulders. Reach the eastern end of Snow Lake at **2.8 miles**. Cross over a stream, then noodle counterclockwise around the lake to a T at **3.0 miles**. It's a big lake, and there are numerous secluded spots along the shore to picnic and swim (although most are taken by noon on sunny Saturdays).

Option

From the T in the trail at 3.0 miles, turn left. You can tell immediately that this trail is used less than the trail up to Snow Lake—it's rougher and narrower. The trail gradually climbs away from the lake. At 5.0 miles, reach Gem Lake. Wildcat Lakes are two miles farther, and even more secluded.

Gazetteer

Nearby camping: Denny Creek Campground
Nearest food, drink, services: Snoqualmie Pass

NOTES:

_____

_____

_____

_____

Hike 26 ⛰️ ⛰️ ⛰️ ⛰️

KENDALL KATWALK

Distance	**11-mile out and back** (14.4-mile option)
Elevation	Low point: 3,000 ft., high point: 5,700 ft., **cumulative gain: 4,200 ft.**
Hike Time	4 to 7 hours, day hike or overnight
Travel	52 miles from Seattle
Season	July through October
Map	Green Trails: *Snoqualmie Pass 207*
Restrictions	NW Forest Pass, dogs on leash, no fires above 4,000 ft., max group 12
More Info	Mt. Baker-Snoqualmie National Forest, Snoqualmie District (North Bend), 425-888-1421, www.fs.fed.us/r6/mbs/

Trail Notes

The Pacific Crest Trail (PCT) heads north from Snoqualmie Pass on its way to the Canadian border, 260 miles distant. It's an awesome route, taking the ridge crests whenever possible. The views, lakes, meadows, and flowers are spectacular. The Kendall Katwalk, a 100-yard section of the PCT etched into a granite cliff 1,200 feet above Silver Creek at the valley floor, is one of the spectacles along the PCT, though it's not really a destination. The hike is long, difficult, and also popular, and the Katwalk may underwhelm you if you've heard too many people gush about it. The necter is in the journey: A peaceful trail, long views, and slanted, rocky meadows prior to and beyond the Katwalk make this a great trip (see Option); the Katwalk is gravy. Note: The Katwalk can also be dangerous, and you shouldn't attempt to cross it in snow.

Driving Directions

From Seattle, drive east on Interstate 90 to Snoqualmie Pass. Take Exit 52. At the end of the exit ramp, set your odometer to zero and turn left. At 0.1 mile, turn right. At 0.2 mile, reach a fork and bear right on Forest Road 9041. Immediately enter the trailhead parking area.

The Kendall Katwalk

The Hike

From the parking area, which is often full on August weekends, the PCT 2000 noodles to the southeast. At **0.2 mile**, the noodling is done as the trail switchbacks up the stout ridge that rises northeast from Snoqualmie Pass. The trail, well worn and nicely graded, climbs up the face of the ridge through evergreen forest.

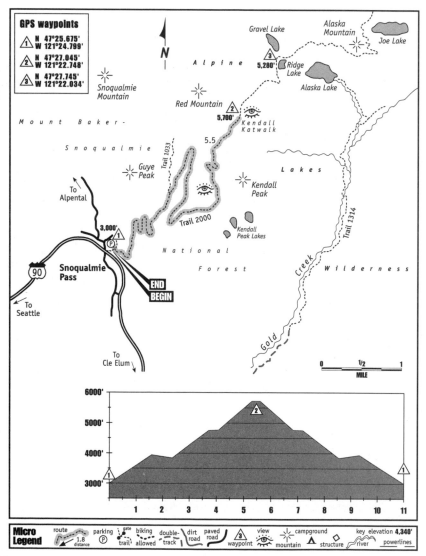

Ridge Lake

At **2.5 miles**, reach a fork and bear right. From here, the trail pulls three excruciatingly long switchbacks as it closes in on the top of the ridge. At **4.3 miles**, the trail tucks in to the west side of the ridge and traverses north. The forest is open here, with small rocky meadows bright with color in August. At **4.8 miles**, the trail switchbacks up to the rocky ridgetop near Kendall Peak and continues north.

At **5.5 miles**, the rocks and meadows disappear and the Katwalk cuts across an open cliff. It's startling and energizing, unless you have vertigo. If that's the case, it's time to turn around.

Option

From the Katwalk, continue north on the PCT to Ridge and Gravel Lakes at the 7.2-mile mark. You'll find fewer people here. There are camp spots at both lakes, and wonderful views from the ridgeline.

Gazetteer

Nearby camping: Denny Creek Campground
Nearest food, drink, services: Snoqualmie Pass

NOTES:

_____

_____

_____

_____

Hike 27 ⛰

SNOQUALMIE TUNNEL

Distance	5.2-mile out and back
Elevation	Low point: 2,500 ft., high point: 2,600 ft., **cumulative gain: 100 ft.**
Hike Time	2 to 4 hours, day hike
Travel	55 miles from Seattle
Season	May through October
Map	Green Trails: *Snoqualmie Pass 207*
Restrictions	State Parks vehicle fee, tunnel closed November through April, day use only, dogs on leash
More Info	Washington State Parks, 360-902-8844, www.parks.wa.gov

Trail Notes

Walking through part or all of the Snoqualmie Tunnel can be a great family adventure. It's flat and short and the cool factor is high, in more ways than one. Bring a jacket and hat because it can get cold in the tunnel, even in the middle of summer. Also, be sure to bring lights to see where you're going. The lights will also alert bicyclists that you're there.

Driving Directions

From Seattle, drive east on Interstate 90 to Exit 54, just over Snoqualmie Pass. At the end of the exit ramp, zero out your odometer and turn right. Immediately turn left, following signs for Iron Horse State Park. At 0.5 mile, turn right, continuing toward Iron Horse State Park. Immediately take another right. At 0.6 mile, reach the trailhead.

The Hike

Facing the trail from the parking area, turn right onto the wide, gravel rail-trail, following the signs to the tunnel. After a short bend in the trail, reach the tunnel entrance at **0.2 mile.**

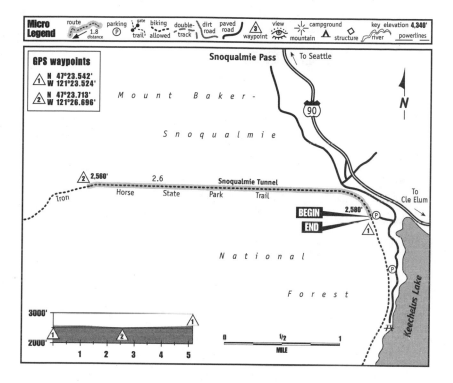

From the tunnel's eastern mouth, you should be able to see a pinpoint of light at the western end of the tunnel, about two-and-a-half miles distant. Click on your light and start walking. As you walk farther in, your pupils will grab for any light. The trail, flat and sometimes wet, stretches ephemerally into the blackness. Reach its western end at **2.6 miles**.

Gazetteer

Nearby camping: Denny Creek Campground
Nearest food, drink, services: Snoqualmie Pass.

NOTES:

Hike 28 ▲ ▲ ▲ ▲

ALASKA LAKE

Distance	10-mile out and back
Elevation	Low point: 2,600 ft., high point: 4,200 ft., **cumulative gain: 1,900 ft.**
Hike Time	4 to 6 hours, day hike or overnight
Travel	57 miles from Seattle
Season	July through October
Map	Green Trails: *Snoqualmie Pass 207*
Restrictions	Dogs on leash, no fires, max group 12
More Info	Mt. Baker-Snoqualmie National Forest, Snoqualmie District (North Bend), 425-888-1421, www.fs.fed.us/r6/mbs/

Trail Notes

Just don't make the mistake of going to Joe Lake. It's only three-quarters of a mile farther and probably more isolated, you think. This is true. But to get to Joe requires lots of pain and agony not unlike putting yourself through a strainer, only the strainer is comprised of young rambunctious vine maples whose job is to impede your way. It's not fun. Trust me. The trip to Alaska Lake is better, near vertical and unmaintained for the last mile, but nothing like the punishment you'll take going to Joe Lake. Alaska Lake is one of the big divots in the huge, gnarled Alpine Lakes Wilderness ridge between Gold Creek valley and the Middle Fork of the Snoqualmie River valley. It's isolated and perfect for a swim on a hot day after the hard climb. The lake also features a nice camp spot. Note: The trail up Gold Creek, though actually inside the Wenatchee National Forest, is administered by the Snoqualmie District of the Mt. Baker-Snoqualmie National Forest.

Driving Directions

From Seattle, drive east on Interstate 90 over Snoqualmie Pass. Take Exit 54. At the end of the exit ramp, set your odometer to zero and turn left. After passing under the interstate, reach a fork at 0.2 mile and turn right, following the sign toward Gold Creek. At 1.1 miles, turn left onto Forest Road 144. Ignore the Gold Creek picnic area on the left at 1.5 miles. At 2.1 miles, ignore driveways on the left and right, and at 2.2 miles, stay to the left as you pass a gated road on the right. At 2.4 miles, park on the left side of the road. The trail begins on the right side.

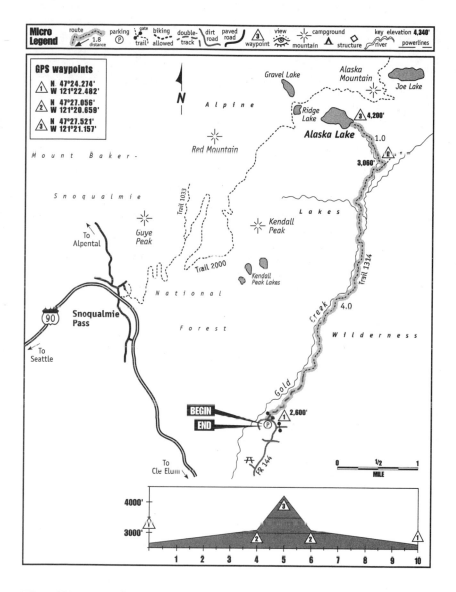

The Hike

The hike begins on private property and you may feel as though you made a wrong turn. Be patient and you'll get there. The route starts out from the trailhead sign on the right side of FR 144, following a gated dirt road. Stay on the main road, ignoring spurs, and you'll reach Trail 1314 at **0.5 mile**. After a short meadowy section, the trail enters an old-growth forest of huge mossy cedars and creviced

Alaska Lake from the Pacific Crest Trail

Douglas firs, and follows Gold Creek, which flows down from Huckleberry Mountain and Chickamin Peak. For the most part, the trail stays along the creek.

At **3.0 miles**, just beyond several campsites, drop into a dry creekbed and look for a rock cairn that marks the next camp. The trail continues through the campsite and into the woods on the opposite side. At **3.2 miles**, ford Gold Creek. Sandals are handy, especially in early summer when the water is high.

Over the next mile, there are two more fords over lesser tributaries. **Whoa!** Just after crossing the second tributary, watch for a cairn that marks an easily missed fork in the trail at **4.0 miles**. Turn left at the fork and follow an unmaintained trail that heads uphill toward Alaska Lake. Uphill, you'll find, is the understatement of the century—you'll climb 1,100 feet over the next mile. On parts of the climb you'll scramble through dense undergrowth, on other parts you'll pick your way across boulder fields. Be patient and watch for cairns that mark the way. **Oof!** At **5.0 miles**, pass over a saddle and arrive at Alaska Lake. It's located in a steep bowl, with slopes, both scree and forested, rising to a ridgeline 1,000 feet above.

Gazetteer
Nearby camping: Denny Creek Campground
Nearest food, drink, services: Snoqualmie Pass

NOTES:

_____

_____

_____

_____

Hike 29 ⛰ ⛰ ⛰

MARGARET LAKE

Distance	6.4-mile out and back
Elevation	Low point: 3,520 ft., high point: 5,180 ft., **cumulative gain: 2,200 ft.**
Hike Time	3 to 4 hours, day hike or overnight
Travel	59 miles from Seattle
Season	July through October
Map	Green Trails: *Snoqualmie Pass 207*
Restrictions	NW Forest Pass, max group 12
More Info	Wenatchee National Forest, Cle Elum District, 509-674-4411, www.fs.fed.us/r6/wenatchee/

Trail Notes

The route to Margaret Lake climbs through clearcuts, with views of Interstate 90 below and more clearcuts across the valley. But in fall, when blueberry and ash turn red and yellow, and the open slopes aren't too hot, it's a pleasant, relatively easy hike over the ridge to Margaret Lake. The lake sits in a small, sparsely forested pocket, with several other lakes nearby. Mountain hemlocks surround camp spots at the southern end, and steep slopes, carved by avalanche chutes in places, shoot up toward Mount Margaret.

Driving Directions

From Seattle drive east on I-90 over Snoqualmie Pass. Take Exit 54. At the end of the exit ramp, set your odometer to zero and turn left. After passing under the interstate, reach a fork at 0.2 mile, and turn right. Stay on the main road, which parallels I-90. At 2.7 miles, the road (Forest Road 4832) switchbacks away from the interstate. At 4.3 miles, reach a fork and bear left on FR 4934. Turn left into the parking area for Trail 1332 at 4.7 miles.

Trail 1332 toward Margaret Lake and Lake Lillian

The Hike

From the parking area, walk back to FR 4934, turn left, and walk up the dirt road. When the road divides at **0.1 mile**, take the lesser fork on the left, following the trail sign. Pass around the broken yellow gate and continue climbing. Exposed to the sun and bright from the rocky tread, this road ascends quickly, and you might feel exhausted after just a half-mile. Stay on the main road, which sways back and forth as it heads northeast toward Mount Margaret.

As the road bends to the right, **0.8 mile**, find a trail on the left marked Hiker Trail and take it. The trail is quite wide, but almost immediately a narrow dirt trail cuts off on the right—take it. From here to the lake you'll be on a narrow trail. To this point, the route has climbed through an old clearcut, and that continues. Through mountain ash and blueberry and small pioneering firs, the trail climbs the southwest flank of Mount Margaret, affording views of Lake Keechelus. At **1.3 miles**, the trail crosses a dirt road.

At **1.9 miles**, the trail leaves the clearcut and enters a mature forest, switchbacking toward the top of the ridge. At **2.4 miles**, the way levels as you gain the ridge and bear north. When you reach a fork at **2.6 miles**—the high point of the hike—turn right, following the sign to Margaret Lake. From here, the trail switchbacks steeply down into a small basin, entering the Alpine Lakes Wilder-

Margaret Lake

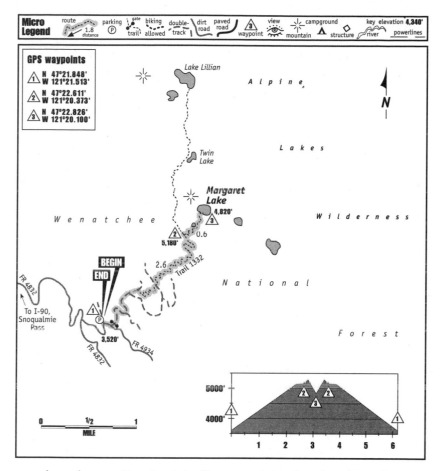

ness along the way. Pass tiny Lake Yvonne at **3.0 miles**, then descend again to reach Margaret Lake at **3.2 miles**.

Gazetteer

Nearby camping: Denny Creek Campground

Nearest food, drink, services: Snoqualmie Pass

NOTES:

Hike 30 ▲ ▲ ▲ ▲

LAKE LILLIAN

Distance	9.2-mile out and back
Elevation	Low point: 3,520 ft., high point: 5,300 ft., **cumulative gain: 3,300 ft.**
Hike Time	4 to 7 hours, day hike or overnight
Travel	59 miles from Seattle
Season	July through October
Map	Green Trails: *Snoqualmie Pass 207*
Restrictions	NW Forest Pass, max group 12
More Info	Wenatchee National Forest, Cle Elum District, 509-674-4411, www.fs.fed.us/r6/wenatchee/

Trail Notes

This sweet mountain lake sits at the southern end of Rampart Ridge. Unofficial trails climb the rock and scree and heathered hillsides north of Lake Lillian in search of routes to Rampart Lakes. Since the way begins through an old clearcut with views of Interstate 90, it's a less popular Alpine Lakes destination than many others, though even here you won't get solitude.

Driving Directions

From Seattle, drive east on I-90 over Snoqualmie Pass. Take Exit 54. At the end of the exit ramp, set your odometer to zero and turn left. After passing under the interstate, reach a fork, 0.2 mile, and turn right. Stay on the main road, which parallels I-90. At 2.7 miles, the road (Forest Road 4832) switchbacks away from the interstate. At 4.3 miles, reach a fork and bear left on FR 4934. Turn left into the parking area for Trail 1332 at 4.7 miles.

The Hike

From the parking area, turn left on FR 4934 and walk up the dirt road. At **0.1 mile**, bear left on a lesser road, following the trail sign. Pass around the broken yellow gate and begin a steep climb. Stay on the main road, which offers little shade as it wends back and forth, heading northeast toward Mount Margaret. At **0.8 mile**, as the road bends to the right, find a trail on the left marked Hiker Trail and take it. The trail is wide at first but almost immediately a narrow dirt trail cuts off on the right—take it.

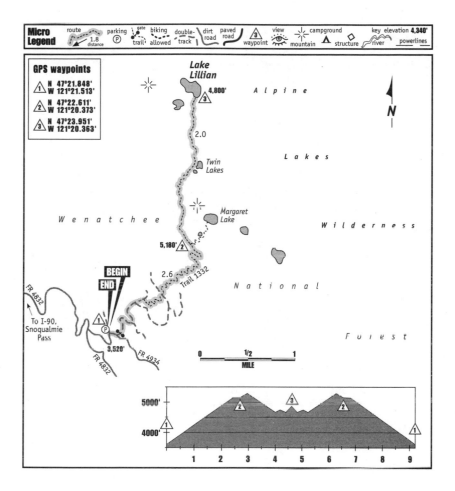

The route continues to climb through the old clearcut. Mountain ash and blueberry and small, pioneering firs cover the southwest flank of Mount Margaret, affording views of Lake Keechelus. At **1.3 miles**, the trail crosses a dirt road. At **1.9 miles**, the trail leaves the clearcut and enters an old-growth forest, switchbacking toward the top of the ridge. At **2.4 miles**, the way levels as you gain the ridge and bear north.

At **2.6 miles**, reach a fork and bear left, continuing along the spine of the ridge (the right fork heads to Margaret Lake, see Hike 29). The trail rounds the west side of Mount Margaret, passing over a high point at **2.9 miles**. From here, the trail drops steadily to a small lakes basin just north of the mountain. Pass by

105

Indian Thistle

Twin Lakes at **3.9 miles**. The trail climbs from the lakes, at times steep and rough. At **4.6 miles**, amid the drama of rocky ridgetops, avalanche chutes, and heather and wildflower-covered slopes, reach Lake Lillian. From the lake, unmaintained trails climb up to Rampart Ridge (see Hike 31) and then on to Alta Mountain.

Gazetteer

Nearby camping: Denny Creek Campground
Nearest food, drink, services: Snoqualmie Pass

NOTES:

Hike 31 ⛰ ⛰ ⛰ ⛰
RAMPART LAKES

Distance	**9.6-mile out and back** (7.6-mile option)
Elevation	Low point: 2,800 ft., high point: 5,180 ft., **cumulative gain: 2,500 ft.**
Hike Time	4 to 7 hours, day hike or overnight
Travel	71 miles from Seattle
Season	July through October
Map	Green Trails: *Snoqualmie Pass 207*
Restrictions	NW Forest Pass, dogs on leash, no fires, max group 12
More Info	Wenatchee National Forest, Cle Elum District, 509-674-4411, www.fs.fed.us/r6/wenatchee/

Trail Notes

This is a surprisingly difficult hike considering its popularity. It's steep and rough, and even during the dry of the summer you'll find yourself carefully stair stepping up huge roots, between sharp rocks, and around pockets of mud. But the forty-car parking area fills up on weekends as hikers challenge Rampart Ridge to see what the fuss is about. Well, the Rampart Lakes basin is something to fuss about. It's a wonderland—puddles, tarns, and small lakes sit on rock- and heather-covered terraces connected by miniature creeks and short, narrow waterways. Unfortunately, crowds have been hard on this subalpine lakes basin. So always stay on the trail, don't build fires, only camp in designated spots, and practice leave-no-trace hiking.

Driving Directions

From Seattle, drive east on Interstate 90. About 10 miles beyond Snoqualmie Pass, take Exit 62. At the end of the exit ramp, set your odometer to zero and turn left. Immediately after crossing over the interstate, go straight through the four-way intersection, bearing slightly to the left. At 5.1 miles, reach a T and turn left onto Forest Road 4930, which is dirt. At 5.5 miles, bear right at the fork, following the signs to Trail 1313. At 9.1 miles, reach the two parking lots that support the trail to Rachel Lake.

The Hike

The trail begins on the opposite side of the road from the parking area. From the sign-in box, the trail at first charges up a few switchbacks, but then levels to follow Box Canyon Creek. Fern and queen's cup, twinflower and Canadian dogwood are scattered throughout the hemlock and fir forest. In several spots, the trail treads across open, brushy avalanche chutes, where grasses and cow parsnip grow five feet tall and tiger lily and columbine somehow manage to compete for space and light. From around the **2-mile** mark, you'll see glimpses through the trees of Rampart Ridge ahead.

At **2.7 miles**, the gradual cant up Box Canyon is over and the serious climbing begins. Over roots and rocks you'll go, occasionally grabbing at the bank or a trailside tree for support. On a warm day, you'll sweat a couple six packs, just to be

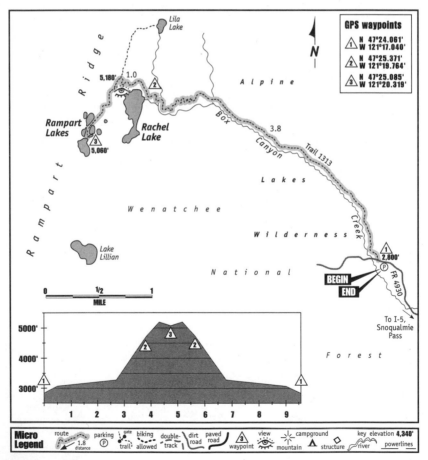

Rachel Lake from Rampart Ridge

sticky enough for the mosquitoes. The switchbacks are tight and unpredictable, scratching for elevation and finding it. Needless to say, this is a tough section.

At **3.8 miles**, the trail levels suddenly and arrives at Rachel Lake. Camp and picnic spots are plentiful on the east side of the lake. The trail kisses the lake and then climbs around the north side, immediately switchbacking up toward the high fin of Rampart Ridge. The trail to the top is at times even steeper than the one below, but without the roots, and the hiking isn't as difficult. The route, in and around the rocky slope past squat mountain hemlock, affords excellent views down to Rachel Lake.

Oof! When you reach an unmarked T, **4.3 miles**, the climb is thankfully over. Turn left at the T. At **4.6 miles**, reach the first water in the Rampart Lakes basin. There's a maze of trails: Don't expand the network of trails by cutting your own. Mountain hemlock and heather populate the space between the rocks and lakes. High rock spines shoot up above the lakes to the west. You'll find the largest of the lakes to the southwest at **4.8 miles**.

Option

The hike to Rachel Lake and back, 7.6 miles, can be a full day, with plenty of elevation and beauty. Turn around at the lake for this shorter hike.

Gazetteer

Nearby camping: Denny Creek Campground
Nearest food, drink, services: Snoqualmie Pass

NOTES:

_____

_____

Hike 32 ⛰ ⛰ ⛰
BOULDER LAKE

Distance	7.6-mile out and back
Elevation	Low point: 1,650 ft., high point: 3,780 ft., **cumulative gain: 2,500 ft.**
Hike Time	3 to 5 hours, day hike or overnight
Travel	58 miles from Seattle
Season	July through October
Map	Green Trails: *Index 142*
Restrictions	Dogs on leash
More Info	Washington State Department of Natural Resources, Northwest Region, 360-856-3500, www.wa.gov/dnr/

Trail Notes

The trail to Boulder Lake is a gradual climb, not easy, but never too steep. Part of the Greider Ridge Natural Resources Conservation Area, the lake is quite nice with good campsites. Stay in the areas provided, however, and only build fires in the steel fire pits. In addition to the Green Trails map listed above, you can get a trail map and brochure at the DNR office in Sedro-Woolley.

Driving Directions

From Seattle, drive northeast on State Highway 522 to Monroe. From Monroe, take US Highway 2 eastbound. About 7.5 miles east of Monroe, pass through the town of Sultan. As you leave Sultan, just past milepost 23, turn left on Sultan Basin Road and set your odometer to zero. You'll pass numerous spurs from this turn to the trailhead: Stay on the main road. At 10.5 miles, the pavement ends. At 13.5 miles, reach a fork and bear right, now on South Shore Road. At 20.7 miles, pass Greider Lakes Trailhead. When the road forks just beyond the trailhead, bear right on DNR Road SL-7000. At 22.0 miles, reach Boulder Lake Trailhead.

The Hike

From the parking area, Boulder Lake Trail heads south, beginning as a doubletrack and slowly narrowing. At **0.25 mile**, cross Boulder Creek on a nice bridge. Afterwards, the route climbs more steeply through a dense forest of alder, fir, and hemlock. **Whoa!** Watch out for nettles trolling for skin along this stretch.

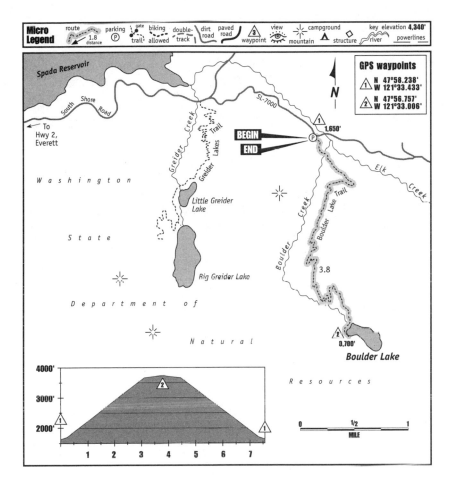

At **0.8 mile**, the trail switchbacks and rounds the low north edge of the ridge. From here, the trail traverses and occasionally switchbacks up the west side of the ridge so the high slope stays on your left and the creek rushes below on your right.

The traverse affords nice views to the west across Boulder Creek valley. A steep, wooded hillside rises to the high rock escarpments that separate Boulder Creek from Greider Lakes (see Hike 33). At about **2.8 miles**, the forest transitions out of the deciduous zone into full evergreen.

At **3.4 miles**, cross a long boardwalk over a marshy meadow that again offers a cool view of rock formations across the valley. The trail levels out a bit here as it

Boulder Lake

reaches for the lake. At **3.8 miles**, arrive at several campsites at the western end of Boulder Lake. On a hot day, a swim after the climb might be just the ticket. Note that sandals are nice for traversing lakeshore rocks. If it's bug season, the swim can serve other purposes as well.

Gazetteer

Nearby camping: Wallace Falls State Park

Nearest food, drink, services: Sultan

NOTES:

_____

_____

_____

_____

Hike 33 ⛰ ⛰ ⛰

BIG GREIDER LAKE

Distance	**5.0-mile out and back**
Elevation	Low point: 1,560 ft., high point: 3,050 ft., **cumulative gain: 1,700 ft.**
Hike Time	2 to 4 hours, day hike or overnight
Travel	57 miles from Seattle
Season	Mid-June through October
Map	Green Trails: *Index 142*
Restrictions	Dogs on leash
More Info	Washington State Department of Natural Resources, Northwest Region, 360-856-3500, www.wa.gov/dnr/

Trail Notes

As the crow flies, it's not much more than a mile from the trailhead to Big Greider Lake, but dozens of switchbacks lengthen the route to 2.5 miles. There are some nice campsites at Big Greider Lake, which lies within the Greider Ridge Natural Resources Conservation Area. In addition to the Green Trails map listed above, you can get a trail map and brochure at the DNR office in Sedro-Woolley.

Driving Directions

From Seattle, drive northeast on State Highway 522 to Monroe. From Monroe, take US Highway 2 eastbound. About 7.5 miles east of Monroe, pass through the town of Sultan. As you leave Sultan, just past milepost 23, turn left on Sultan Basin Road and set your odometer to zero. You'll pass numerous spurs from this turn to the trailhead: Stay on the main road. At 10.5 miles, the pavement ends. At 13.5 miles, reach a fork and bear right, now on South Shore Road. At 20.7 miles, reach Greider Lakes Trailhead on the right.

Near the egress of Big Greider Lake

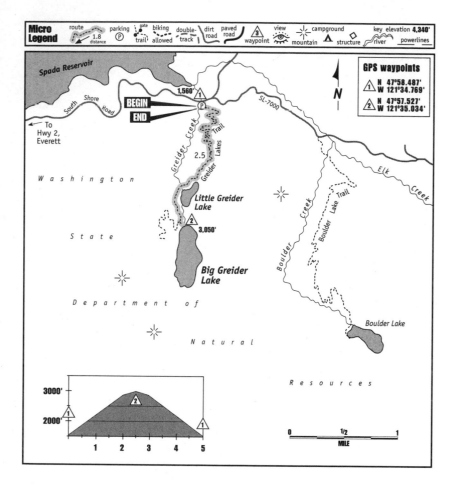

The Hike

From the parking area, Greider Lakes Trail noodles through the open, some-times brushy lowlands at the bottom of Greider Creek. But at **0.2 mile**, the trail bolts up the hillside toward the Greider Lakes basin. An astonishing number of switchbacks zigzag directly south up the steep, forested slope.

At **1.6 miles**, the punishing set of switchbacks ends and the trail traverses around the ridge to the southwest. At **2.0 miles**, reach Little Greider Lake. From here, the trail winds around the western shore of the lake, then crosses Greider Creek. You'll climb a bit after the creek crossing, then traverse across a steep, open slope before descending to the north tip of Big Greider Lake. Green slopes on all

Big Greider Lake

sides cup the large lake and climb 1,500 feet to a series of high ridge points. At **2.5 miles**, reach a fork and bear left, dropping down to the lake. The right fork, a faint, brushy route, climbs another half-mile to the top of a precipitous overlook that affords views of the lake and surrounding area.

Gazetteer

Nearby camping: Wallace Falls State Park
Nearest food, drink, services: Sultan

NOTES:

_____

_____

_____

_____

Hike 34 ▲ ▲ ▲
WALLACE FALLS ✓

Distance	**6.6-mile loop** (5.4-mile option)
Elevation	Low point: 320 ft., high point: 1,540 ft., **cumulative gain: 2,000 ft.**
Hike Time	3 to 4 hours, day hike
Travel	42 miles from Seattle
Season	April through November
Map	Green Trails: *Index 142*
Restrictions	State Parks vehicle fee, day use only, dogs on leash
More Info	Washington State Parks, 360-902-8844, www.parks.wa.gov

Trail Notes

The Woody Trail up to several viewpoints of Wallace Falls is lovely and quite popular, and of course the falls are spectacular. Most people take the hike as an out and back. However, you can form a loop by returning via a trail along an old logging railroad bed, which is also lovely but much less traveled, and that's the way I've described it here. Due to state parks funding cuts, the parking area at Wallace Falls is closed on Mondays and Tuesdays from October through March. The trails are open, though probably muddy, on these days. Park on the Gold Bar side of the short bridge noted in the driving directions. Whenever the parking fills up on sunny weekends during the rest of the year, you'll have to park there too. To park in the lot you'll need a state parks parking permit.

Driving Directions

From Seattle, drive north on Interstate 405 then northeast on State Highway 522 to Monroe. From Monroe, take U.S. Highway 2 eastbound. About 13.5 miles east of Monroe, enter the town of Gold Bar. Just before milepost 28 in Gold Bar, turn left onto First Street and set your odometer to zero. At 0.4 mile, turn right onto May Creek Road. When the road forks at 1.2 miles, bear to the left onto Ley Road, following the signs to Wallace Falls State Park. Cross a small bridge. At a 4-way at 1.6 miles, take the middle route. At 1.8 miles, reach the parking area for Wallace Falls State Park. Note: If the parking area is full, and it often is on summer weekends, you'll need to drive back and park alongside the road—tires off the pavement—on the Gold Bar side of the small bridge.

The Hike

From the parking area, walk east on a wide gravel trail—an access road really—that runs beneath a set of power lines. After about **0.4 mile**, the wide trail breaks to the left into the trees and immediately forks. Take Woody Trail, the right fork, toward Wallace Falls. It's a hiker-only trail from here to the falls. At **0.6 mile**, bear to the right at the fork. The tread is dark, rich, and root-strewn. Bear right each time as you reach other forks at **1.2 miles** and at **1.5 miles**. Drop to a bridge over North Fork Creek, and then begin a much steeper ascent.

Wallace Falls

Reach the first falls viewpoint and picnic shelter at **1.7 miles**. Continuing up the trail, you'll find three more viewpoints. At **2.3 miles**, arrive at the next to last view of the falls. You may want to turn around here: The final pitch of trail to the upper viewpoint is very steep, and the tangle of roots makes the going difficult. Reach the top and a view of the falls from above at **2.7 miles**. Turn around here and descend past the views of the falls and the shelter to the bridge over North Fork Creek. Cross the bridge and climb to a fork at **3.9 miles**—turn right (stay to the left for the shorter option).

The trail climbs away from the rush of Wallace River. At **4.2 miles**, reach a wide trail—an old logging railroad grade—and turn left, gradually descending through a forest of alder, cedar, hemlock, and fir. This upper trail is more lonesome than the busy Woody Trail. At **5.0 miles**, reach a fork at a kiosk and bear left again. The wide trail descends more quickly from here. At **6.2 miles**, reach a fork and bear right, popping out of the

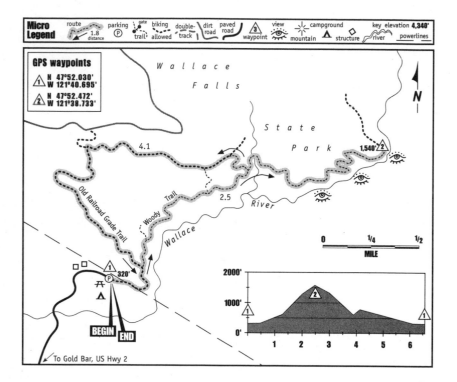

woods and joining the access road under the power lines. At **6.6 miles**, reach the parking area.

Option

For the shorter, 5.4-mile option, stay to the left at 3.9 miles, following the Woody Trail back the way you came.

Gazetteer

Nearby camping: Wallace Falls State Park
Nearest food, drink, services: Gold Bar

NOTES:

Hike 35 ⛰ ⛰ ⛰
LAKE SERENE

Distance	**7.2-mile out and back**
Elevation	Low point: 580 ft., high point: 2,560 ft., **cumulative gain: 2,200 ft.**
Hike Time	3 to 5 hours, day hike
Travel	48 miles from Seattle
Season	July through October
Map	Green Trails: *Index 142*
Restrictions	NW Forest Pass, no camping, no fires
More Info	Mt. Baker-Snoqualmie National Forest, Skykomish District, 360-677-2414, www.fs.fed.us/r6/mbs/

Trail Notes

This is a popular trail, with Bridal Veil Falls and Lake Serene, both spectacular, competing for top billing. Bridal Veil Creek cascades over the rocks in countless streams and sprays and shoots all the way from the lake. The creek drops about 1,300 feet in less than one-half mile, and it's in free-fall for much of that distance. Lake Serene is equally dramatic. Sparsely forested on the north tip, most of the lake sits cupped by sheer rock cliffs that church-spire up to the rocky points of Mount Index rising 3,500 feet above. The trail's northern aspect means that

snow lingers to July in many years despite the fact that the lake lies at only 2,500 feet. Though the trail is steep and root-strewn, well-maintained switchbacks and stairs made of wood rounds make the climb hikable and not too rugged.

Driving Directions

From Seattle, drive northeast on State Highway 522 to Monroe. From

Lake Serene in June

Monroe, turn right on US Highway 2 and head east. About 21 miles east of Monroe, just past milepost 35, turn right on Mount Index Road (Forest Road 6020). Zero out your odometer here. At 0.3 mile, reach a fork and go right on FR 6020-109. At 0.4 mile, find the trailhead parking on the left.

The Hike

From the parking area, walk up the road and around the gate. When the road forks at **0.1 mile**, bear right, following the hiker sign. The rocky roadway ends at a creek, amid a light, lush forest of alder and salmonberry. Across the creek, the trail is narrow at first, but then widens. At **0.4 mile**, cross the creek again. The trail climbs moderately, at times rocky, then sandy; at times narrow, then wide.

At **1.2 miles**, reach a fork and bear right, again following the hiker sign. The trail here is five feet wide or more. Reach another fork at **1.3 miles**, and this time go left. At **1.4 miles**, reach a fork and bear left, descending. (A right here climbs one-half mile to a closeup view of Bridal Veil Falls.) Follow a set of stairs down to a stream crossing at **1.6 miles**, where you'll find a great view of the falls from below.

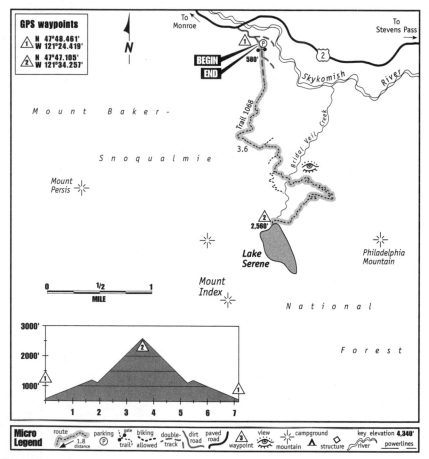

Then up, up, up you'll climb on a granite staircase, passing from a mixed forest of alder into the coniferous dark on the steep lower slopes of Philadelphia Mountain. You'll climb into vertigo-land, with cedar, fir, and hemlock swirling about you, and dizzying views into the alder forest below lit by blotchy spirals of olive-colored moss.

Oof! Just past the **3.0-mile** mark, after innumerable switchbacks, the trail turns back to the west and traverses, gaining elevation but at a more gradual rate. It's here also that the route emerges from the thick woods of the lower slopes and crosses the bright north exposure to the lake. A final push over

Bridal Veil Falls

the lip of the bowl reveals Lake Serene at **3.6 miles**, somewhat larger and quite a bit more dramatic than expected, with rock cliffs that verily shoot up from the southern shore of the lake toward the stark rocky heights of Mount Index.

Gazetteer
Nearby camping: Money Creek Campground
Nearest food, drink, services: Index, Gold Bar

NOTES:

_____

_____

_____

_____

Hike 36 ⛰

BARCLAY LAKE

Distance	4.2-mile out and back
Elevation	Low point: 2,240 ft., high point: 2,440 ft., **cumulative gain: 500 ft.**
Hike Time	2 to 3 hours, day hike
Travel	54 miles from Seattle
Season	July through October
Map	Green Trails: *Monte Cristo 143*
Restrictions	NW Forest Pass, no camping, no fires
More Info	Mt. Baker-Snoqualmie National Forest, Skykomish District, 360-677-2414, www.fs.fed.us/r6/mbs/

Trail Notes

The walk to Barclay Lake is perhaps the easiest hike included here—it's short, there's almost no elevation gain, and the trail's in good condition. On sunny days, the lake will sparkle as the precipitous north wall of Baring Mountain looms above.

Driving Directions

From Seattle, drive northeast on State Highway 522 to Monroe. From Monroe, turn right on US Highway 2 and head east. About 27 miles east of Monroe, just past milepost 41, turn left on Forest Road 6024. Zero out your odometer at the turn. In quick succession, cross a set of railroad tracks then proceed straight through a four-way intersection. At 4.6 miles, the road ends at the trailhead.

The Hike

Trail 1055 toward Barclay Lake meanders, but never really climbs, along the southern bank of Barclay Creek. From the start, you can see the north wall of Baring Mountain—a huge rock monolith—looming through the trees to the southeast. The forest is semi-dense, with pockets of old growth; the rush of the creek is in the air.

Boardwalk to Barclay Lake

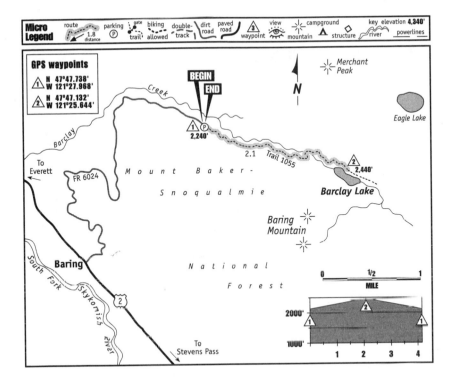

Follow the smooth trail across several boardwalks. Though there are rocky sections, and a broken log bridge over Barclay Creek farther on, it's an easy, pleasant walk through the woods. Cross the creek at about **1.6 miles**. More quickly than expected, reach the day-use area at Barclay Lake at **2.0 miles**. From the picnic area, the trail follows the north shore of the lake, and you'll find another picnic area about half-way down the lake, **2.1 miles**.

Gazetteer

Nearby camping: Money Creek Campground

Nearest food, drink, services: Index, Gold Bar

NOTES:

_____

_____

_____

_____

Hike 37 ⛰️⛰️⛰️⛰️

BLANCA LAKE

Distance	**7.8-mile out and back**
Elevation	Low point: 1,900 ft., high point: 4,650 ft., **cumulative gain: 3,500 ft.**
Hike Time	3 to 6 hours, day hike or overnight
Travel	65 miles from Seattle
Season	July through October
Map	Green Trails: *Monte Cristo 143*
Restrictions	NW Forest Pass, max group 12
More Info	Mt. Baker-Snoqualmie National Forest, Skykomish District, 360-677-2414, www.fs.fed.us/r6/mbs/

Trail Notes

I've got to say that Blanca is one badass lake. Blanca is big and phenomenally dramatic, dramatic beyond belief, with sheer 2,000-foot cliffs that shoot up from its eastern shore. The Columbia Glacier—tucked between Columbia and Monte Cristo Peaks—feeds the lake from the north, and Blanca's outlet, Troublesome Creek, plunges 2,000 feet in the first mile and throws up a roar during snowmelt that will raise the hair on the back of your neck. Of course badass isn't always so

Playing at Blanca Lake, with Columbia Glacier in the distance

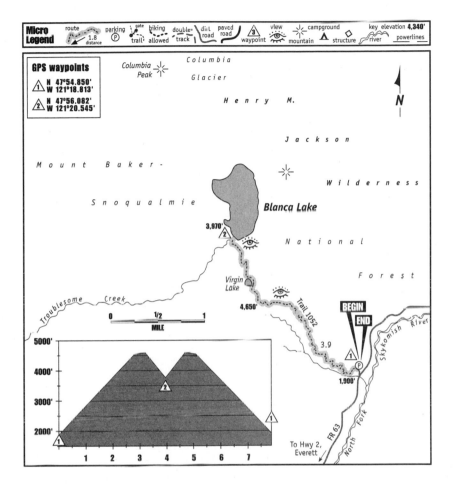

easy to get to (though it is popular). The 2,700-foot climb to the saddle above Virgin Lake is quite strenuous, but the trail is good, with few roots or rocks. Beyond the saddle, though, as you pass into the Henry M. Jackson Wilderness, the root-packed trail cants wrongly as it drops, headlong at times, down to the Blanca Lake, keeping the hair up on your neck the whole way.

Driving Directions

From Seattle, drive northeast on State Highway 522 to Monroe. From Monroe, take US Highway 2 eastbound. About 21 miles east of Monroe, past milepost 35, turn left on North Fork Road (Forest Road 63) toward Index. Zero out your odometer at this turn. At 0.9 mile, stay to the right, passing the bridge into Index on your left. At 11.5 miles, pass Troublesome Creek Campground on the right. Pass San Juan Campground a few miles later. At 14.3 miles, bear left at the fork. At 15.2 miles, reach another fork and turn left to stay on FR 63, which is now dirt. Stay on the main road. At 17.2 miles, reach a fork and go left toward Blanca Lake Trail. Arrive at the trailhead at 17.3 miles.

The Hike

Blanca Lake Trail 1052 begins easy, graveled and wide, but after about a quarter mile, that's the end of that. Enjoy that first easy jaunt, because from there on the trail charges up the hillside, gaining elevation as fast as you can count mosquitoes at Peek-a-boo Lake (see Hike 57). There are a few roots, but for the most part the trail is in good shape considering the acute angle of ascent. The forested slope, an eastern wrinkle in Troublesome Mountain's forehead, sports cedar, hemlock, fir, and the occasional vine maple. Higher up the relentless climb, mountain hemlock appears.

Oof! The climb eases at **2.9 miles**. As you near the saddle, you can see Glacier Peak through the trees to the right. As you enter the wilderness, just after cresting the saddle at **3.2 miles**, you'll see Virgin Lake below, which is small and almost exactly round. Follow the trail around the right side of Virgin Lake and then down. The trail is wide and easy for a few hundred yards, then trouble. Roots and mud and a few fallen trees conspire with the steep slope to make the going difficult. At **3.6 miles**, the trail crosses through a tiny rock meadow, then drops down through a rockfall to the lake, **3.8 miles**. As the lake appears, the view is impressive, almost outrageous, and hard to capture in your head all at once.

Gazetteer

Nearby camping: San Juan Campground, Troublesome Creek Campground
Nearest food, drink, services: Index

NOTES:

_____

_____

_____

_____

Hike 38 ⛰️ ⛰️
LAKE DOROTHY

Distance	**6.0-mile out and back** (longer options)
Elevation	Low point: 2,200 ft., high point: 3,820 ft., **cumulative gain: 950 ft.**
Hike Time	4 to 8 hours, day hike or overnight
Travel	70 miles from Seattle
Season	July through October
Map	Green Trails: *Skykomish 175*
Restrictions	NW Forest Pass, no dogs, max group 12
More Info	Mt. Baker-Snoqualmie National Forest, Skykomish District, 360-677-2414, www.fs.fed.us/r6/mbs/

Trail Notes

Here's one of the more popular Alpine Lakes Wilderness hikes off US Highway 2. It's relatively short with a moderate elevation gain, quite lovely, and often crowded. But since Dorothy lays claim to being one of the largest lakes in the Alpine Lakes, measuring over one and a half miles in length, and the trail continues on to three more beautiful mountain lakes—Bear, Deer, and Snoqualmie—you should be able to find a secluded spot to enjoy lunch and a moment of reflection as you take in the backcountry views.

Driving Directions

From Seattle, drive northeast on State Highway 522 to Monroe. From Monroe, take US Highway 2 eastbound. About 33 miles east of Monroe, immediately before a tunnel, turn right and follow the Money Creek Campground signs. Set your odometer to zero here. Cross the South Fork of the Skykomish River, pass the campground, and stay on the main road bearing left. At 1.0 mile, turn right on Miller River Road (Forest Road 6410). Almost immediately, stay left on FR 6410. The road becomes gravel a quarter-mile farther. At 6.7 miles, cross a one-lane bridge. At 10.5 miles, reach the trailhead and park.

The Hike

The trail, rocky and root-strewn from the start, gradually climbs a hillside, humping south. The East Fork of the Miller River flows below on the right. Enter the Alpine Lakes Wilderness. After about **0.5 mile**, descend to a wood bridge over Camp Robber Creek near its confluence with the East Fork. After following a series of stepping stumps and a lengthy boardwalk, the trail gradually leaves the river and meanders uphill through the woods. A round of steady switchbacks climbs east toward the northern head of Lake Dorothy.

At **2.0 miles**, reach the small logjam at the river's source. The trail forks just before the logjam—bear left. **Whoa!** This turn is easily missed. Climb several hundred feet above the lake on another set of stepping stumps, traverse the slope, then descend back to the lakeshore again.

The trail continues across a boardwalk. Pass several campsites and pit toilets as you make your way south along the east side of Lake Dorothy, **3.0 miles**. This makes for a good picnic spot and turnaround.

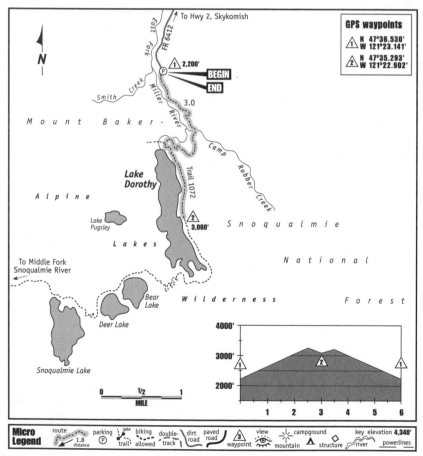

Lake Dorothy

Option

From the 3-mile mark about midway down Lake Dorothy's length, the trail continues south. Reach the south end of the lake at 4.0 miles. From there, the trail crosses several creeks before climbing over a ridge and descending to Bear Lake, 5.3 miles. Still looking to get farther away and add more miles to your boots? From Bear Lake the trail continues on to Deer Lake then Snoqualmie Lake over the next mile.

Gazetteer

Nearby camping: Miller River Campground
Nearest food, drink, services: Skykomish

NOTES:

Hike 39 ⛰ ⛰ ⛰ ⛰

BIG HEART LAKE

Distance	**13.6-mile out and back** (3.0- and 7.5-mile options)
Elevation	Low point: 1,640 ft., high point: 4,940 ft., **cumulative gain: 4,500 ft.**
Hike Time	5 to 9 hours, day hike or overnight
Travel	70 miles from Seattle
Season	Mid-July through mid-October
Map	Green Trails: *Skykomish 175*
Restrictions	NW Forest Pass, no dogs, no fires, max group 12
More Info	Mt. Baker-Snoqualmie National Forest, Skykomish District, 360-677-2414, www.fs.fed.us/r6/mbs/

Trail Notes

Get a little backcountry love by hiking into the heart of the Alpine Lakes Wilderness. Sure it's a long way to Big Heart Lake, but you'll pass four other lovely (and substantial) mountain lakes on the way—Trout, Malachite, Copper, and Little Heart—and the scenery on the route is outstanding. This is more of a traditional overnight trek than day hike, especially considering the significant elevation gain, but if you are going for just the day, start early so you can really enjoy the love.

Driving Directions

From Seattle, drive northeast on State Highway 522 to Monroe. From Monroe, take US Highway 2 eastbound. About 36 miles east of Monroe, pass the Skykomish Ranger Station on the left and set your odometer to zero. At 0.6 mile, turn right on Foss River Road Northeast (Forest Road 68). At 1.8 miles, just after a one-lane bridge, bear right at a fork, following the sign toward West Fork Foss River Trail. It's here that the road turns to dirt. At 4.2 miles, bear right at the fork to continue on FR 68, and at 4.9 miles, pass by a trailhead. At 5.5 miles, bear left at the fork onto FR 6835, following the sign toward Trail 1064. The road ends at the trailhead, 7.5 miles.

The Hike

The trail, which begins rocky and wide like a creek bed, almost immediately enters the Alpine Lakes Wilderness. Gradually, the trail smoothes out then crosses

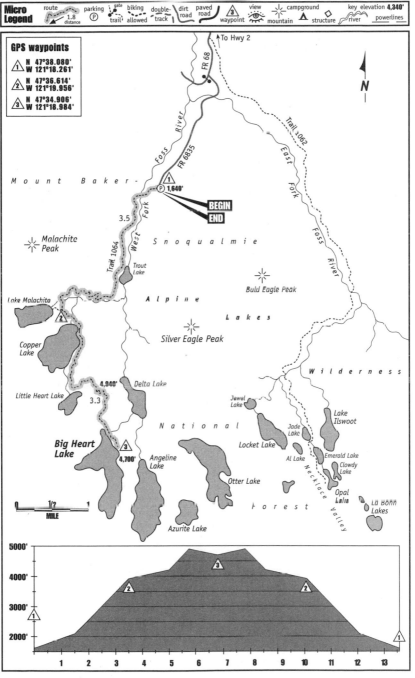

Copper Lake

the West Fork of the Foss River at **0.5 mile**. The trail follows the river, climbing steadily toward Trout Lake.

Pass Trout Lake on the left at **1.5 miles**. There's a campsite here, as well as a day-use area and a toilet. Beyond the lake, the trail bends to the west, away from the river, and begins to climb more and more steeply. As you climb, you'll parallel the creek that pours from Lake Malachite down into West Fork Foss River, and you'll pass two waterfalls. Oof! It's a tough climb. At **3.3 miles**, the trail bends to the south and crosses the creek. At **3.5 miles**, reach a fork and bear left. (The right fork spurs up to Lake Malachite, one-quarter mile away.)

After a short distance, pass a small pond on the right, cross a creek, and then arrive at Copper Lake. The trail curls around the eastern shore. About halfway down the lake, the trail eases away from the water and climbs gently south to Little Heart Lake. Reach Little Heart Lake at **5.0 miles**. From here, climb east and then south, crossing a high shoulder of the ridge between Little Heart Lake and Big Heart Lake. Gain the high point of the route at **5.7 miles**. The trail cuts to the right here and traverses under a small summit before descending down to Big Heart Lake. Reach the camp area at the lake at **6.8 miles**.

Option

Let's face it: 13.6 miles is a long way for a day hike. If you're just out for the day and aren't up for a forced-march-into-the-wilderness outing, turn around at Trout Lake (roundtrip 3.0 miles) or take the spur trail on the right to Lake Malachite at the 3.5-mile mark, reaching the lake at 3.75 miles (roundtrip 7.5 miles).

Gazetteer

Nearby camping: Beckler River Campground
Nearest food, drink, services: Skykomish

NOTES:

_____

_____

Hike 40 ▲ ▲ ▲ ▲

NECKLACE VALLEY

Distance	16.4-mile out and back
Elevation	Low point: 1,680 ft., high point: 4,780 ft., **cumulative gain: 3,500 ft.**
Hike Time	6 to 11 hours, day hike or overnight
Travel	68 miles from Seattle
Season	Mid-July through mid-October
Maps	Green Trails: *Skykomish 175, Stevens Pass 176*
Restrictions	NW Forest Pass, no dogs, no fires, max group 12
More Info	Mt. Baker-Snoqualmie National Forest, Skykomish District, 360-677-2414, www.fs.fed.us/r6/mbs/

Trail Notes

It would be a challenge to count all the lakes in the Alpine Lakes Wilderness, and the Necklace Valley is Exhibit One. It's lovely up there, the rocky ledges and postage-stamp meadows, wildflowers and craggy peaks. And the lakes. This is also a very challenging day hike, especially after the river crossing, and many hikers take one or two days each way. It's the best way to enjoy this treasure.

Driving Directions

From Seattle, drive northeast on State Highway 522 to Monroe. From Monroe, take US Highway 2 eastbound. About 36 miles east of Monroe, pass the Skykomish Ranger Station on the left and set your odometer to zero. At 0.6 mile, turn right on Foss River Road Northeast (Forest Road 68). At 1.8 miles, just after a one-lane bridge, bear right at a fork, continuing on FR 68, which is now dirt. Stay on the main road. At 4.2 miles, bear right at the fork to continue on FR 68. At 4.9 miles, reach the trailhead for the Necklace Valley Trail 1062 on the left.

The Hike

Necklace Valley Trail 1062 heads up the East Fork of the Foss River, ascending easily to the south. At **1.5 miles**, enter the Alpine Lakes Wilderness. The trail, riffing melodiously across numerous tributaries, stays to the east of the river. It's a lovely mixed forest with big trees and lush valley-floor undergrowth. Sections of the trail may be overgrown, so watch out for dangling nettles.

After kissing the East Fork Foss River a few times, the trail finally crosses to

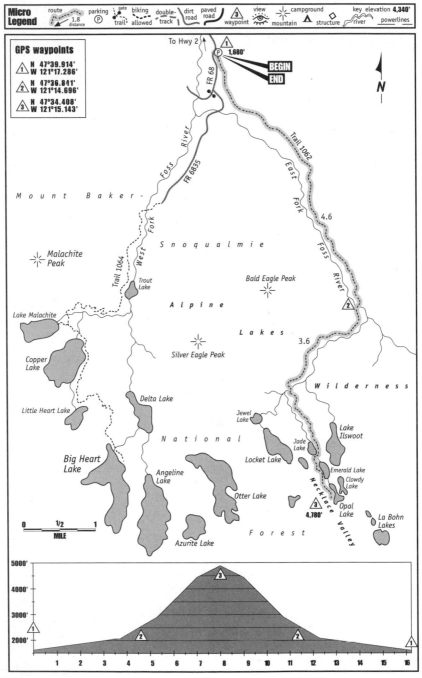

Tiger lily and fern

the west side of the river at **4.6 miles** (it seems a particularly long 4.6 miles). From here, the route leaves the river and bears west as it follows a creek that pours down from the lakes in the Necklace Valley. Follow the cairns up a short but very steep and difficult boulder field. Over the first five miles, the trail gains a paltry 700 feet—it's relatively easy going. But beyond this river crossing, the difficulty ratchets up as the trail climbs the steep, narrow valley squeezed between Bald Eagle and Silver Eagle Peaks to the west and Mount Hinman to the southeast. The tread roughens considerably too; it is loose in places, rocky, and root-strewn.

Oof! At about **6.0 miles**, the trail breaks to the south again, still climbing but with less arduous focus. At **6.6 miles**, with most of the rough-going past, cross the creek. Just beyond the **7-mile** mark, you'll pop through a narrow gap and reach Jade Lake, the first Necklace Valley lake. The trail rounds Jade Lake to the east, wraps around the south end, and approaches Emerald Lake from the west. The official, maintained trail ends at the south end of Opal Lake, **8.2 miles**, however numerous climbing trails, some marked by cairns, head up to the myriad nearby lakes and tarns, peaks and high vistas.

Gazetteer

Nearby camping: Beckler River Campground
Nearest food, drink, services: Skykomish

NOTES:

_____

_____

_____

_____

Hike 41 ⛰ ⛰ ⛰ ⛰
PEAR LAKE

Distance	17-mile out and back
Elevation	Low point: 2,000 ft., high point: 5,280 ft., **cumulative gain: 3,950 ft.**
Hike Time	6 to 13 hours, day hike or overnight
Travel	74 miles from Seattle
Season	July through mid-October
Map	Green Trails: *Benchmark Mountain 144*
Restrictions	NW Forest Pass, max group 12
More Info	Mt. Baker-Snoqualmie National Forest, Skykomish District, 360-677-2414, www.fs.fed.us/r6/mbs/

Trail Notes

The trail along Meadow Creek, into the Henry M. Jackson Wilderness, toward Fortune Mountain and the Pacific Crest Trail, seems to take a long time to get anywhere. That's just the point. Sure the climb from Fortune Ponds over to Pear Lake is dramatic—rock crags, gnarled mountain hemlock, clinging wildflowers—but the lonesome trek up along Meadow Creek is the thing here, all six plus miles of it. It's a long way to the trailhead, there's no official parking, and the trail goes on forever. That's the recipe for keeping a trail quiet and wonderful. So if you're up for a long hike and want some quiet, head for Pear Lake.

Driving Directions

From Seattle, drive northeast on State Highway 522 to Monroe. From Monroe, take U.S. Highway 2 eastbound. About 34 miles east of Monroe (0.5 mile past milepost 49), turn left on Beckler River Road (Forest Road 65) and set your odometer to zero. At 7.1 miles, just as the road becomes dirt, reach a four-way intersection. Take a soft right turn onto FR 6530. At 11.6 miles, find the trail on the left side of the road. There's no real parking area, and FR 6530 is narrow, so choose your spot carefully.

Junction with the Pacific Crest Trail

The Hike

Right from the dirt road, Trail 1057 charges up the hillside, gaining 1,000 feet over the first mile. The trail is hard packed and quite narrow with some embedded rocks. This is a lesser-used trail, and it can be brushy on the first mile if it hasn't been recently maintained. At **1.5 miles**, the serious incline eases somewhat, and the trail traverses north, following Meadow Creek. The forest is deeper and more mature here, and the trail less brushy and enclosed.

At **2.6 miles**, pass into the Henry M. Jackson Wilderness. Continue north on this traverse for quite a distance, staying above the creek to the east. At **3.9 miles**, the trail drops to Meadow Creek and crosses over to the west side, and then hugs the creek. At **4.7 miles**, you'll cross back to the east side of the creek and climb away from it, ascending the western flank of Fortune Mountain.

At **5.4 miles**, the trail bends north again, traversing, and winds around the mountain's midsection. Crest a lightly forested high point and descend into a basin that cups Fortune Ponds. For day hikers, this is a good

Trail ascends the north side of Fortune Mountain

place to picnic with a turnaround in mind. At **6.8 miles**, the trail wraps around the ponds bearing right. **Whoa!** There are several other trails here, so be sure to bear right and climb steeply before crossing the little creek. From here, the trail ascends at an arduous rate into the subalpine zone. The way is rocky and steep. Soon after you gain the saddle at **7.3 miles**, you can see Pear Lake below. The trail

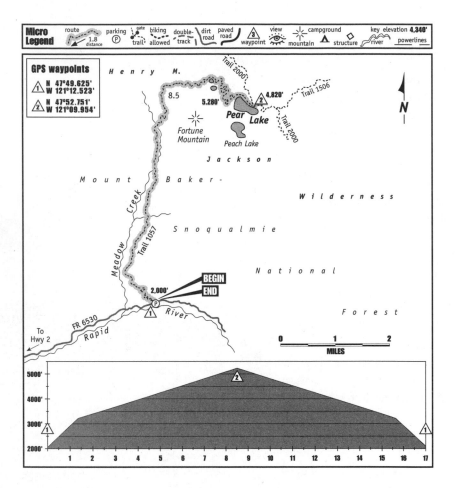

seems to do kick turns down the steep rock face. Reach the lake at **8.3 miles**. At **8.5 miles**, rendezvous with the Pacific Crest Trail.

Gazetteer

Nearby camping: Beckler River Campground
Nearest food, drink, services: Skykomish

NOTES:

Hike 42 ⛰ ⛰ ⛰
SURPRISE CREEK

Distance	8-mile out and back
Elevation	Low point: 2,240 ft., high point: 4,500 ft., **cumulative gain: 2,400 ft.**
Hike Time	3 to 5 hours, day hike or overnight
Travel	72 miles from Seattle
Season	Mid-July through October
Map	Green Trails: *Stevens Pass 176*
Restrictions	NW Forest Pass, dogs on leash, no fires, max group 12
More Info	Mt. Baker-Snoqualmie National Forest, Skykomish District, 360-677-2414, www.fs.fed.us/r6/mbs/

Trail Notes

The trailhead for Surprise Creek brings to mind of all the hustle bustle you're trying to escape—the roar of the highway, the ding-ding of the railroad, and the crackle of power lines above. But after just a few minutes of walking, you'll enter the Alpine Lakes Wilderness, and soon you'll only hear the gurgle of Surprise Creek (and the conversations of other hikers) as you climb the long valley toward the lakes basin to the south. After mounting the head of the valley, you'll find Surprise Lake surrounded by Surprise, Spark Plug, and Thunder Mountains. Be sure to linger, enjoying the quiet, before returning.

Driving Directions

From Seattle, drive northeast on State Highway 522 to Monroe. From

Columbine in bloom

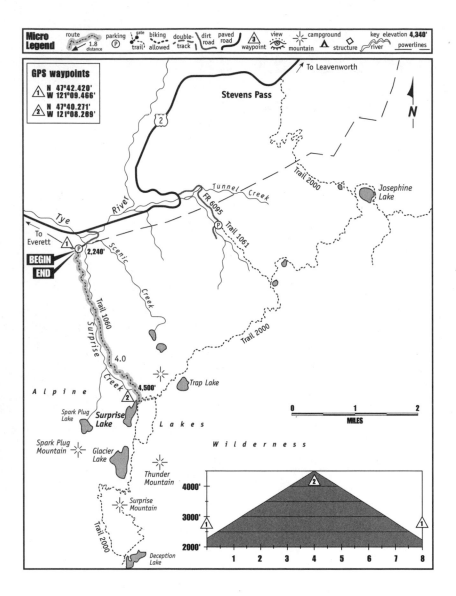

Monroe, take US Highway 2 eastbound. About 43 miles east of Monroe, past milepost 58, turn right onto Forest Road 840 and set your odometer to zero. This turnoff is not well signed. FR 840 bears left, drops to cross Tye River, then crosses a set of railroad tracks. From the tracks, bear right to stay on the main road, ignoring spurs to the left. At 0.4 mile, the road ends at the trailhead.

Surprise Lake

The Hike

From the trailhead, hike south, away from the powerlines, on Surprise Creek Trail 1060. The route parallels the creek, aiming south up the tight valley. At **0.3 mile**, cross into the Alpine Lakes Wilderness. After the **0.5-mile** point, the trail runs very close to the creek. At **1.2 miles**, cross to the east side of the creek, and continue up the moderate grade, still alongside the creek.

At **2.6 miles**, at the southern head of the valley, the trail ascends more steeply, throwing in a few sharp switchbacks for good measure. At **4.0 miles**, reach a fork in the trail and the north end of Surprise Lake.

Gazetteer

Nearby camping: Money Creek Campground

Nearest food, drink, services: Skykomish

NOTES:

_____

_____

_____

_____

Hike 43 ⛰ ⛰ ⛰ ⛰
THUNDER MOUNTAIN

Distance	**11.6-mile one way** (15.5-mile loop option)
Elevation	Low point: 2,240 ft., high point: 5,820 ft., **cumulative gain: 4,500 ft.**
Hike Time	5 to 10 hours, day hike or overnight
Travel	74 miles from Seattle
Season	Mid-July through October
Map	Green Trails: *Stevens Pass 176*
Restrictions	NW Forest Pass, dogs on leash, no fires, max group 12
More Info	Mt. Baker-Snoqualmie National Forest, Skykomish District, 360-677-2414, www.fs.fed.us/r6/mbs/

Trail Notes

This Thunder Mountain half-loop offers a little bit of Pacific Crest Trail (PCT) love, but no good suggestion for completing the loop. The love: Trail 2000 between Hope Lake and Glacier Lake is classic PCT, bopping along the high ridgeline with wildflowers ablaze and spectatular views around every bend. The loop: Unfortunately, the route ends 3.9 miles of dirt road and Highway 2 walking from the starting point. So you'll have to shuttle cars, hitch-hike, or slog out those 3.9 miles to make this route work out. Hey, love ain't cheap.

Driving Directions

From Seattle, drive northeast on State Highway 522 to Monroe. From Monroe, take US Highway 2 eastbound. About 45 miles east of Monroe, just past

milepost 60, turn right onto Forest Road 6095 and set your odometer to zero. After crossing Tunnel Creek, bear right at the fork to stay on FR 6095. At 0.6 mile, bear left at the fork. Reach the trailhead for Tunnel Creek Trail at 1.2 miles.

The Hike

Tunnel Creek Trail 1061 climbs south at a healthy rate, through fir and hemlock, up to Hope Lake and its junction with the Pacific Crest Trail. At **1.6 miles**, after 1,100 feet of climbing, reach a T at Hope Lake,

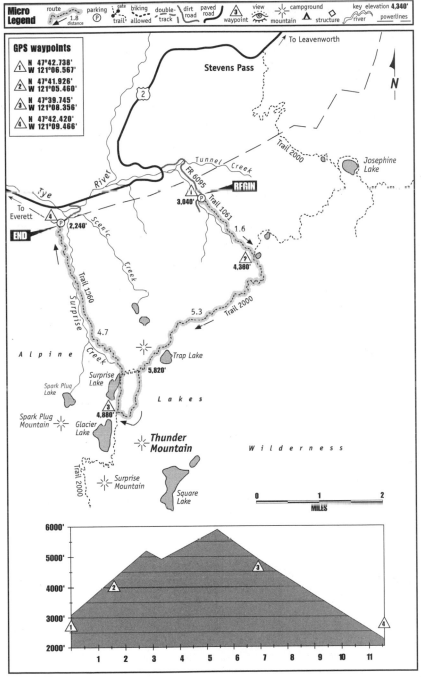

Micro Legend

route · 1.8 distance · parking (P) · gate · trail · biking allowed · double-track · dirt road · paved road · 3 waypoint · view mountain · campground · structure · key elevation **4,340'** · river · powerlines

GPS waypoints

⚠1 N 47°42.738'
W 121°06.567'

⚠2 N 47°41.926'
W 121°05.460'

⚠3 N 47°39.745'
W 121°08.356'

⚠4 N 47°42.420'
W 121°09.466'

To Leavenworth

Stevens Pass

2

Trail 2000

Josephine Lake

Tunnel Creek

FR 6095

Tye River

Scenic Creek

BEGIN

3,040'

Trail 1061

1.6

2 4,360'

To Everett

END

2,240'

Trail 1060

Surprise Creek

5.3

Trail 2000

4.7

Alpine

5,820'

Trap Lake

Spark Plug Lake

Surprise Lake

L a k e s

Spark Plug Mountain

Glacier Lake

3 4,880'

Thunder Mountain

W i l d e r n e s s

Trail 2000

Surprise Mountain

Square Lake

0   1   2
MILES

6000'
5000'
4000'
3000'
2000'

1 2 3 4 5 6 7 8 9 10 11

Trap Lake

a tiny puddle really. The ridge it sits on is significant, though, sending water flowing down its north slope into the Skykomish River, and runoff flowing down its south slope into the Wenatchee River. Turn right at the T, and immediately enter the Alpine Lakes Wilderness, heading south on the PCT toward Trap and Surprise Lakes.

A ridgeline trail for much of its 2,600-mile route, the PCT heads south and mounts the high ridge above Trapper Creek. It's a tough, sometimes rocky climb from Hope Lake up the ridge. At **2.8 miles** the trail levels out, then winds and picks its way along the south side of the ridge, much of it through open hillside meadow. In late July and August, the wildflowers along this stretch of trail are magnificent—tiger lily and columbine, paintbrush and thistle, all swaying in a light breeze.

At **4.9 miles**, pass Trap Lake below on the left, then climb to a saddle. Crest the high point at **5.2 miles**. Beyond the saddle, the trail drops steeply to a fork, **5.6 miles**. Turn left here, following the PCT toward Glacier Lake. From the junction, the trail heads directly south, straight at the impressive north face of Thunder Mountain. The trail descends and gradually veers to the west. At **6.9 miles**, reach a T next to a tiny lake—turn right. From Glacier Lake, at the foot of Thunder Mountain, hike north. Pass by Surprise Lake on the left. At **7.6 miles**, at the north end of Surprise Lake, reach a fork and bear left, heading down Trail 1060 along Surprise Creek. The trail runs right along the creek as it drops 2,300 feet over the next four miles. At **11.6 miles**, reach the Surprise Creek Trailhead. If you didn't shuttle a car or meet a friend on the trail to give you a life, it's 3.9 miles farther around to the start.

Gazetteer

Nearby camping: Money Creek Campground
Nearest food, drink, services: Skykomish

NOTES:

Hike 44 ⛰ ⛰ ⛰
JOSEPHINE LAKE

Distance	**10-mile out and back**
Elevation	Low point: 4,060 ft., high point: 5,120 ft., **cumulative gain: 2,500 ft.**
Hike Time	4 to 6 hours, day hike or overnight
Travel	77 miles from Seattle
Season	Mid-July through October
Map	Green Trails: *Stevens Pass 176*
Restrictions	NW Forest Pass, dogs on leash, no fires, max group 12
More Info	Mt. Baker-Snoqualmie National Forest, Skykomish District, 360-677-2414, www.fs.fed.us/r6/mbs/

Trail Notes

If you're not going to hike the Pacific Crest Trail (Trail 2000), from Mexico to Canada, you might at least spend a day hiking it up to Josephine Lake from Stevens Pass. It's a tough up-and-down hike, exposed to the sun parts of the way, but it's often the start of a big hike, southwest to Snoqualmie Pass or southeast toward Mount Stuart.

Driving Directions

From Seattle, drive northeast on State Highway 522 to Monroe. From Monroe, take US Highway 2 eastbound to Stevens Pass, about 49 miles farther. At the pass, pull into the ski area's large gravel parking area on the right. The trail begins from the upper lot to the east of the buildings.

The Hike

The Pacific Crest Trail 2000 begins by winding southward up through the Stevens Pass Ski Area—not the most beautiful start to a mountain hike. The route, sometimes dusty and hot, crosses several ski runs and swings in and out of old-growth forest. At **1.8 miles**, cross over a high point at the top of a ski lift and begin switchbacking down the south side of the ridge

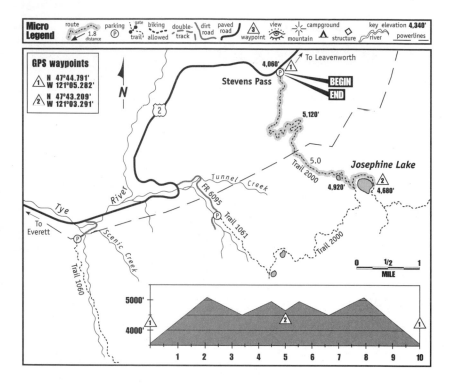

through open talus. At **2.3 miles**, still descending, cross a road and then pass under three sets of powerlines.

Beyond the powerlines, the trail levels out. The route begins an easy climb around **3.4 miles**. At **3.9 miles**, reach Lake Susan Jane. From the lake, the trail climbs steeply up to a saddle. At **4.5 miles**, just beyond the saddle, reach a fork above Josephine Lake: Take the trail on the left that traverses around the far side of the lake, gradually descending down to the shore and a campsite, **5.0 miles**.

Gazetteer

Nearby camping: Money Creek Campground
Nearest food, drink, services: Skykomish

NOTES:

Hike 45 ⛰ ⛰ ⛰ ⛰
LAKE VALHALLA

Distance	10.8-mile out and back
Elevation	Low point: 3,760 ft., high point: 5,060 ft., **cumulative gain: 2,000 ft.**
Hike Time	4 to 6 hours, day hike or overnight
Travel	77 miles from Seattle
Season	Mid-July through October
Maps	Green Trails: *Stevens Pass 176, Benchmark Mountain 144*
Restrictions	NW Forest Pass, dogs on leash, no fires, max group 12
More Info	Wenatchee National Forest, Lake Wenatchee/Leavenworth District, 509-763-3103, www.fs.fed.us/r6/wenatchee/

Trail Notes

The route from Stevens Pass to Lake Valhalla via the Pacific Crest Trail (Trail 2000) isn't the shortest way to reach the lake, but it's a nice way. (If you drive around to Forest Road 6700, the trail via Union Gap is less than three miles.) The climb, much of it through the Henry M. Jackson Wilderness, is mostly gentle to moderate.

Driving Directions

From Seattle, drive northeast on State Highway 522 to Monroe. From Monroe, take US Highway 2 eastbound to Stevens Pass, about 49 miles farther. Imme-

A rainy day on the Pacific Crest Trail

diately over the pass, pull into the large gravel parking area on the left. The trail begins near a small A-frame building near the back of the parking area.

The Hike

The Pacific Crest Trail 2000 heads northeast from behind the substation. To begin, the trail follows the route of an old road, traversing northeast on a gradual descent. It's open here, affording long views down the Nason Creek valley. At **1.7 miles**, the trail bears left, leaves the noise of the highway behind, and begins climbing. Soon you're in old-growth forest. The trail is well maintained and the climb is mostly gradual.

Cross over a small creek at **2.3 miles**. Soon afterward, you'll pass into the Henry M. Jackson Wilderness. From here, the trail traverses around the north

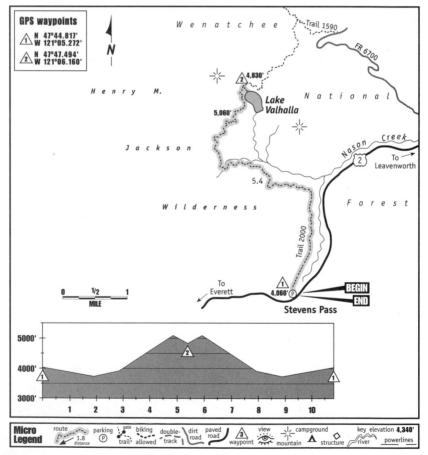

Lake Valhalla

side of a ridge, staying low near the creek and heading west. After a few steep switchbacks, the trail breaks to the north. Ignore a lesser spur trail on the left, **3.8 miles**, that leads to a sometimes pond. The way becomes steeper here, climbing over roots and a few rocks, and zigzagging up the ridge that holds Lake Valhalla.

At **4.9 miles**, pop over the top of the ridge. The descent from the ridgetop is rough, rocky, and muddy. But as you drop through mountain hemlock and fir, you'll glimpse the lake down to the right. The descent sets you down in a meadow near the north end of the lake where you'll reach a fork, **5.3 miles**. Turn right and arrive at the lakeshore at **5.4 miles**.

Gazetteer

Nearby camping: Money Creek Campground
Nearest food, drink, services: Skykomish

NOTES:

_____

_____

_____

_____

Hike 46 ⛰ ⛰ ⛰

MOUNT PILCHUCK

Distance	6-mile out and back
Elevation	Low point: 3,120 ft., high point: 5,320 ft., **cumulative gain: 2,400 ft.**
Hike Time	3 to 5 hours, day hike
Travel	57 miles from Seattle
Season	Mid-July through mid-October
Map	Green Trails: *Granite Falls 109*
Restrictions	NW Forest Pass, dogs on leash, day use only
More Info	Mt. Baker-Snoqualmie National Forest, Darrington District (Verlot), 360-691-7791, www.fs.fed.us/r6/mbs/

Trail Notes

The hike up Mount Pilchuck is quite popular, and for good reason. Though steep and somewhat rocky, it's a relatively short hike, and the views from the old fire lookout at the summit are simply incredible. With the crowds and the views in mind, plan this trip for a sunny weekday. The hike begins in the Mt. Baker-Snoqualmie National Forest, and since they manage most aspects of this trail, a NW Forest Pass is required and their contact information is above. However, most of the trail is actually in Mount Pilchuck State Park (800-233-0321).

Lookout atop Mount Pilchuck

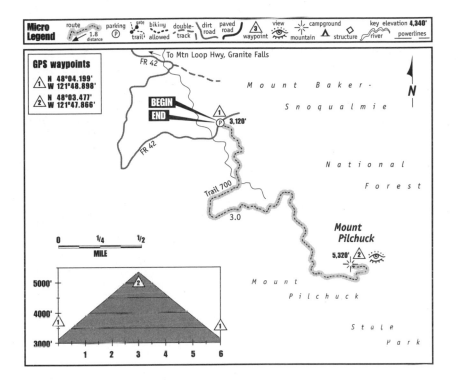

Driving Directions

From Everett, go east on US Highway 2, then east on State Highway 204, then north on State Hwy 9, and finally east on State Hwy 92 to Granite Falls, where State Hwy 92 becomes Stanley Street. Pass through Granite Falls, then turn left on Mountain Loop Highway toward Monte Cristo. Zero out your odometer here. At 12.0 miles, just after a bridge, turn right on Forest Road 42 toward Mount Pilchuck. At 19.2 miles, reach the Mount Pilchuck Trailhead and park.

The Hike

Mount Pilchuck Trail 700 climbs gradually out away from FR 42, heading south through a fir, hemlock, and cedar forest. At **0.7 mile**, ford a small creek and enter Mount Pilchuck State Park. The ascent is steeper now. At around **1.1 miles** skirt a clearcut on the right. From here, you'll find the tread rougher and the ascent even steeper.

The trail crosses a talus slope, switchbacks, and continues an uphill traverse. At **1.6 miles**, the trail veers to the right and climbs straight up a face to a saddle between two minor summits. After crossing between the two high points, the trail

151

Exploring Mount Pilchuck's fire lookout

contours to the left and crosses the south flank of Mount Pilchuck, climbing gently up to the ridgeline. **Whoa!** Snow can linger into August, and while climbing straight up the boulder field looks like the fast route, it can lead to a skull-cracking fall.

After gaining the high, meadowed ridgeline just east of the summit, follow the trail as it switchbacks to the west and climbs. Reach the summit and the old fire lookout at **3.0 miles**. The views are awesome, and the series of lakes to the east lovely.

Gazetteer

Nearby camping: Turlo Campground, Verlot Campground
Nearest food, drink, services: Granite Falls

NOTES:

_____

_____

_____

_____

Hike 47

HEATHER LAKE

Distance	4-mile out and back
Elevation	Low point: 1,400 ft., high point: 2,500 ft., **cumulative gain: 1,300 ft.**
Hike Time	2 to 3 hours, day hike or overnight
Travel	52 miles from Seattle
Season	Mid-June through October
Map	Green Trails: *Granite Falls 109*
Restrictions	NW Forest Pass, dogs on leash
More Info	Mt. Baker-Snoqualmie National Forest, Darrington District (Verlot), 360-691-7791, www.fs.fed.us/r6/mbs/

Trail Notes

Heather Lake sits in a basin surrounded by steep rock that reaches up toward Mount Pilchuck. In early summer, waterfalls cascade down the cliffs across the lake. The snow clears from this beautiful, short trail before most other hikes found off the Mountain Loop Highway. Though popular and well maintained, this trail has some sections that are steep, rocky, and root-strewn. A number of nice picnic spots frame the lake, as well as a few choice campsites.

Driving Directions

From Everett, go east on US Highway 2, then east on State Highway 204, then north on State Hwy 9, and finally east on State Hwy 92 to Granite Falls, where State Hwy 92 becomes Stanley Street. Pass through Granite Falls, then turn left on Mountain Loop Highway. Set your odometer to zero. At 12.0 miles, immediately after a bridge, turn right on Forest Road 42 toward Mount Pilchuck. At 13.4 miles, find the parking area for Heather Lake Trail on the right.

The Hike

The trail begins on the opposite side of the road from the small parking area. Right from the get-go, Heather Lake Trail 701, rocky and root-strewn, climbs and switchbacks south into a dark forest, thick with fir and hemlock and the

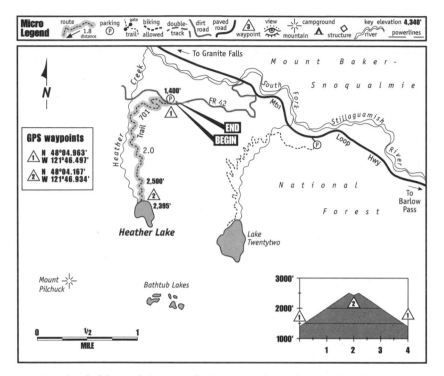

occasional red alder and vine maple. In spots, the understory is rich, green, and ferned; in others the thick forest remains dark, even on the brightest days, and the undergrowth is spare. After a few switchbacks, **0.4 mile**, the trail joins an old, rocky roadbed and, counterintuitively, begins descending. After a few minutes, you'll bear to the left, following the trail sign, and resume the climb.

On the way up, numerous tiny but insistent creeks make the rocks slick, and the footing sometimes precarious. The trail swings west and traverses toward Heather Creek. Around **0.8 mile**, you'll hear the rush of the creek below on the right. The climb eases at **1.5 miles**, crosses an easily gained high point in the forest, then gradually descends to the lake, **2.0 miles**.

Gazetteer

Nearby camping: Turlo Campground, Verlot Campground

Nearest food, drink, services: Granite Falls

NOTES:

Hike 48 ⛰ ⛰ ⛰
LAKE TWENTYTWO

Distance	**5.4-mile out and back**
Elevation	Low point: 1,100 ft., high point: 2,540 ft., **cumulative gain: 1,550 ft.**
Hike Time	2 to 4 hours, day hike
Travel	52 miles from Seattle
Season	Mid-June through October
Maps	Green Trails: *Granite Falls 109, Silverton 110*
Restrictions	NW Forest Pass, day use only, no dogs, no fires
More Info	Mt. Baker-Snoqualmie National Forest, Darrington District (Verlot), 360-691-7791, www.fs.fed.us/r6/mbs/

Trail Notes

The trail to Lake Twentytwo has somewhat of a split personality, as if maintained to two very different standards. It begins wide, graveled, and easy, winding through a lush, broad, low valley forest. Then it becomes steep, rocky, and awkward, protected from the elements by only spindly vine maples. One thing's for sure, though, it's a popular trail, especially early in the season when the higher trails are still in snow. I saw 12 people and 5 dogs—a no-no—before 10 a.m. on a very rainy Saturday morning.

Lake Twentytwo Creek

Driving Directions

From Everett, go east on US Highway 2, then east on State Highway 204, then north on State Hwy 9, and finally east on State Hwy 92 to Granite Falls, where State Hwy 92 becomes Stanley Street. Pass through Granite Falls, then turn left on Mountain Loop Highway toward Monte Cristo. Zero out your odometer here. At 13.1 miles, turn right onto the short spur to the trailhead for Lake Twentytwo.

The Hike

The trail, which is wide and graveled to begin, heads west from the parking area and meanders through lush forest and over rushing creeks. At **0.6 mile**, the trail bends to the left around a broad tongue of ridge and bears south. It's here that the switchbacks and climbing begin in earnest. It seems as though every other switchback reveals an interesting but partially obscured waterfall along the creek that drains the lake above.

After a few more switchbacks, the trail leaves the huge trees that mark the lowlands here and obscure the cascading water to zigzag up a boulder field. The

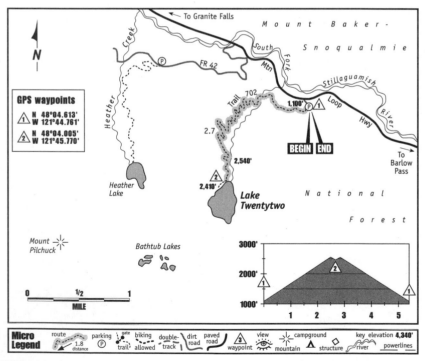

Rain on Lake Twentytwo

trail here is much more difficult for hiking than the wide, gravel and dirt switchbacks below. And without much tree cover, save the low reaching vine maples that have pioneered out into the rocks, it can be a hot stretch on a sunny day. The boulder field is slow going, steep and awkward.

At **2.4 miles**, leave the hot, exposed boulder field and reenter the woods. After crossing an easy rise, the trail drifts down to Lake Twentytwo, **2.7 miles**.

Gazetteer

Nearby camping: Turlo Campground, Verlot Campground
Nearest food, drink, services: Granite Falls

NOTES:

_____

_____

_____

_____

Hike 49 🔺🔺🔺

CUTTHROAT LAKES

Distance	6.8-mile out and back
Elevation	Low point: 3,120 ft., high point: 4,180 ft., **cumulative gain: 3,400 ft.**
Hike Time	3 to 5 hours, day hike or overnight
Travel	64 miles from Seattle
Season	July through October
Map	Green Trails: *Silverton 110*
Restrictions	Dogs on leash
More Info	Washington State Department of Natural Resources, Northwest Region, 360-856-3500, www.wa.gov/dnr/

Trail Notes

The trail to Cutthroat Lakes is named for its trail builder, Walt Bailey, who spent years building trail in the bold topography between Mallardy Ridge and

Bald Mountain, sustained by the search for pools and lakes and small meadows that open unexpectedly to the hiker's delight. You'll hit lots of ups and downs, some steep though the trail is generally smooth, a small meadow here, a densely forested hillside there, and little streams lined with marsh marigolds in late spring. If you think the way up sounds nice, wait until you arrive at the tarns and small lakes that make up the Cutthroat Lakes Basin. Firewood is scarce near the lakes and fires may be prohibited in the future, so if you camp use a stove. Note: There's only room for a few cars at the trailhead; if that spot is full, look for a few wideish spots in the road a short way back.

Marsh marigold in springtime

Driving Directions

From Everett, go east on US Highway 2, then east on State Highway 204, then north on State Hwy 9, and finally east on State Hwy 92 to Granite Falls, where State Hwy 92 becomes Stanley Street. Pass through Granite Falls, then turn left on Mountain Loop Highway toward Monte Cristo. Zero out your odometer

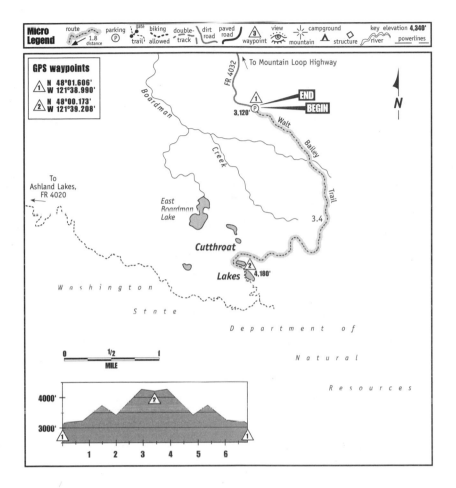

here. At 11.0 miles, pass the Verlot Ranger Station. At 18.2 miles, immediately before crossing the South Fork of the Stillaguamish at Red Bridge, turn right on Forest Road 4030, a paved, one-lane road. At 19.5 miles, bear right at the fork, taking FR 4032, which is gravel. Stay on the main road. At 25.3 miles, the road ends at the small trailhead.

The Hike

From a berm at the end of the road, the Walt Bailey Trail hugs the steep west side of Mallardy Ridge, heading south. Narrow and choppy in places, the trail cuts a traversing ascent. Firs and hemlocks open up occasionally to offer views down to the right into Boardman Creek valley. Just beyond the **1.0-mile** mark, the trail levels and crosses one of the upper trickles of Boardman Creek. In June, marsh marigolds bloom along the muddy banks while the snow melts around them, acting as heralds to July's wild bouquet, when insects abound to pollinate the small meadow. This is the first in a series of small and wonderful meadows the trail crosses on the way to Cutthroat Lakes.

Near Cutthroat Lakes

From the first meadow, the trail climbs around the side of a steep draw, then passes through another meadow, and so on. Dropping and climbing, it winds through fir and hemlock only so long as to find another meadow to linger in and wend across. At **2.5 miles**, the trail climbs the face of a broad ridge that holds Cutthroat Lakes. It's a sharp ascent, gaining over 500 feet in less than half a mile. From the top, the trail winds through open meadows, with heather and mountain hemlock filling the rocky cracks. To the east, Big Four Mountain and Sperry and Vesper Peaks show impressively. Reach the second and slightly larger Cutthroat Lake at **3.4 miles**.

Gazetteer

Nearby camping: Gold Basin Campground
Nearest food, drink, services: Granite Falls

NOTES:

_____

_____

_____

_____

Hike 50 ⛰ ⛰ ⛰ ⛰

MOUNT FORGOTTEN MEADOWS

Distance	7.8-mile out and back
Elevation	Low point: 2,100 ft., high point: 5,000 ft., **cumulative gain: 3,000 ft.**
Hike Time	3 to 6 hours, day hike
Travel	65 miles from Seattle
Season	Mid-July through mid-October
Map	Green Trails: *Sloan Peak 111*
Restrictions	NW Forest Pass, no camping, dogs on leash
More Info	Mt. Baker-Snoqualmie National Forest, Darrington District (Verlot), 360-691-7791, www.fs.fed.us/r6/mbs/

Trail Notes

The Perry Creek Trail is often used as an approach to Mount Forgotten by climbers eager to bag another Mountain Loop Peak. But the hike description here won't take you to the summit. It won't take you to a high mountain lake either. This trail points the way to a series of high meadows that expose a panorama of rocky, snow-capped peaks. Rocky and brushy in sections, and almost always steep, the trail crosses talus slopes, passes Perry Creek Falls, runs through old-growth forest, and emerges at the top, into wonderful wildflower meadows.

Driving Directions

From Everett, go east on US Highway 2, then east on State Highway 204, then north on State Hwy 9, and finally east on State Hwy 92 to Granite Falls, where State Hwy 92 becomes Stanley Street. Pass through Granite Falls, then turn

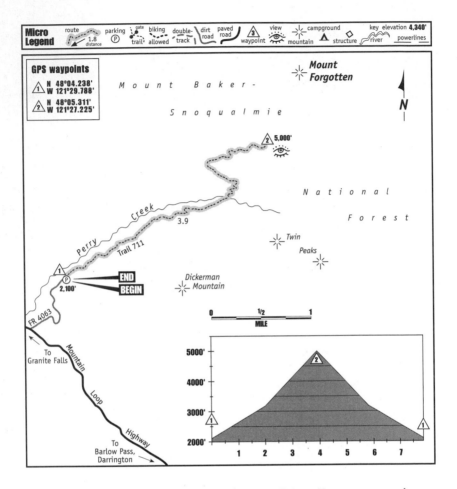

left on Mountain Loop Highway toward Monte Cristo. Zero out your odometer here. At 11.0 miles, pass the Verlot Ranger Station. At 26.5 miles, turn left toward Perry Creek Trail onto Forest Road 4063. At 27.5 miles, the road terminates at the parking area for Perry Creek Trail.

The Hike

Perry Creek Trail 711 immediately enters an evergreen forest and begins a steady climb. As the trail traverses up the valley, with the creek below to the north, the forest opens up. You'll cross a series of talus slopes, which can be brushy. At **1.9 miles**, reach Perry Creek Falls. It's hard to get a good look at the falls, but the roar from the base and the partial views provide excellent waterfall fodder for your imagination.

Perry Creek Trail

Just above the falls, the trail crosses Perry Creek, heads north, and begins switchbacking. Gone are the steep talus traverses of the north side of the valley. The duff trail is smooth through the big-tree forest, but the way is steep here— nearly a thousand feet per mile—and it feels as though each step burns many tens of calories. At **3.7 miles**, pass a picnic spot where the trail meets up with the ridgeline. Continue up the trail as it follows the ridge. At **3.9 miles**, reach Forgotten Meadows. The meadows, filled with wildflowers in July, afford incredible views of Dickerman Mountain to the south, Big Four across the valley, and Glacier Peak through the gap between Mount Forgotten and Twin Peaks.

Gazetteer

Nearby camping: Gold Basin Campground

Nearest food, drink, services: Granite Falls

NOTES:

_____

_____

_____

_____

_____

Hike 51 ⛰ ⛰ ⛰ ⛰ ⛰

DICKERMAN MOUNTAIN

Distance	**8.6-mile out and back**
Elevation	Low point: 1,980 ft., high point: 5,720 ft., **cumulative gain: 3,820 ft.**
Hike Time	4 to 7 hours, day hike
Travel	65 miles from Seattle
Season	Mid-July through mid-October
Map	Green Trails: *Sloan Peak 111*
Restrictions	NW Forest Pass, dogs on leash
More Info	Mt. Baker-Snoqualmie National Forest, Darrington District (Verlot), 360-691-7791, www.fs.fed.us/r6/mbs/

Trail Notes

Also often referred to as Mount Dickerman, this is a peak for the peak baggers. It's steep and the switchbacks are relentless, but the payoff is big—sweet, high alpine meadows and views from Oregon to Alaska. Or so it seems. Watch out, though, there's no water available on this hike and significant portions are exposed to the sun.

Driving Directions

From Everett, go east on US Highway 2, then east on State Highway 204, then north on State Hwy 9, and finally east on State Hwy 92 to Granite Falls, where State Hwy 92 becomes Stanley Street. Pass through Granite Falls, turn left on Mountain Loop Highway toward Monte Cristo, and zero out your odometer. At 11.0 miles, pass the Verlot Ranger Station. After 27.8 miles on Mountain Loop Hwy, turn left into the small trailhead parking for Dickerman Mountain.

From Dickerman Mountain, Twin Peaks and Glacier Peak beyond

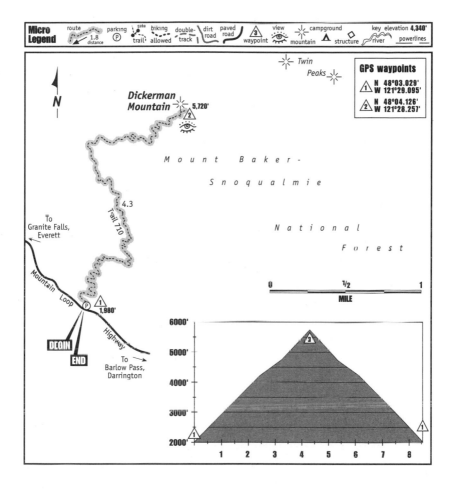

The Hike

The Dickerman Mountain Trail 710 starts out by cutting to the right, then gently climbing within sight of the Mountain Loop Highway, through a shaded forest of big trees. After about **0.2 mile**, though, switchbacks begin ascending the steep south slope of the mountain in bounds rather than baby steps. And there's not much letup. From here, a shifting, rocky tread demands careful hiking.

Around **2.5 miles**, the trail cross a narrow gully and exits the dark forest. Now the climb is more gradual, meandering through small groves of subalpine fir. At about **3.2 miles**, the trail meets up with a sharp ridgeline, and the summit is visible above to the northeast. From here, the trail is nearly shadeless for the re-

165

Dickerman Mountain

mainder of the climb, affording long views south but allowing little respite from the sun on a hot day. Follow the ridge for a short distance, then drop east of the ridgeline through a series of small, rocky meadows.

Tight switchbacks approach the summit from the south slope, through meadows ablaze in wildflowers and full of huckleberry. **Oof!** Reach the summit at **4.3 miles**. Spectacular views will spin you around from the big volcanoes to the south to Glacier Peak to the north, and numerous Mountain Loop peaks in between.

Gazetteer

Nearby camping: Gold Basin Campground

Nearest food, drink, services: Granite Falls

NOTES:

_____

_____

_____

_____

Hike 52 ⛰ ⛰ ⛰ ⛰
GOTHIC BASIN

Distance	**9.4-mile out and back**
Elevation	Low point: 2,360 ft., high point: 5,000 ft., **cumulative gain: 3,050 ft.**
Hike Time	4 to 6 hours, day hike or overnight
Travel	68 miles from Seattle
Season	Mid-July through mid-October
Maps	Green Trails: *Sloan Peak 111, Monte Cristo 143*
Restrictions	NW Forest Pass, dogs on leash
More Info	Mt. Baker-Snoqualmie National Forest, Darrington District (Verlot), 360-691-7791, www.fs.fed.us/r6/mbs/

Trail Notes

Standing in Gothic Basin, even in mid-July, can resemble being knee-deep in the cratered middle of a cookies and cream ice cream cone—and as the sun beats down you can be hot and cold at the same time. That's the image and I'm sticking to it. Between Sheep Gap Mountain to the south and Gothic and Del Campo Peaks to the north, wide snowfield ribbons mix with bouldered slopes, cirques, and sheer rock cliffs, and waterfalls plunge into icy lakes. The trip up to the basin is just over 4 miles, but much of the route is open and exposed, and the trail is very steep, rough in spots, and occasionally dangerous. An ice axe is recommended until mid-August.

Driving Directions

From Everett, go east on US Highway 2, then east on State Highway 204, then north on State Hwy 9, and finally east on State Hwy 92 to Granite Falls, where State Hwy 92 becomes Stanley Street. Pass through Granite Falls, then turn left on Mountain Loop Highway. Set your odometer to zero. At 11 miles, pass the Verlot Ranger Station. At 30.8 miles, just before the road turns to dirt at Barlow Pass, turn left into the parking area for the hike to Monte Cristo.

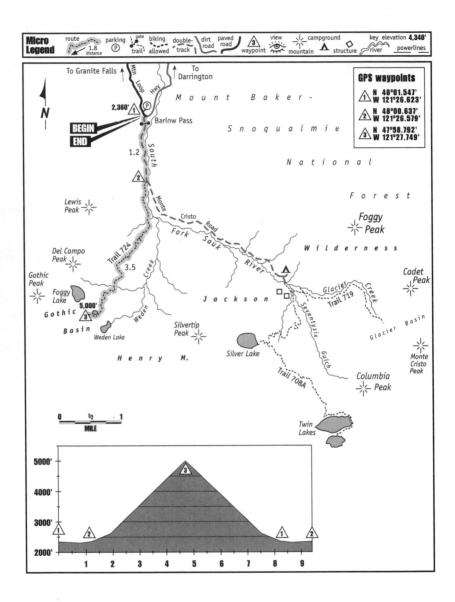

The Hike

The hike to Gothic Basin begins with a walk along the road to Monte Cristo, which begins on the other side of the road from the parking area. Carefully cross Mountain Loop Hwy, pass around a gate, and head south on Monte Cristo Road. The way is flat and uninspired as it follows the South Fork of the Sauk River. At about **1.2 mile**, just before crossing Twin Bridge, find Weden Creek Trail on the right—take it.

Trail 724 follows the river at a distance on an easy traverse. At **1.9 miles**, the trail begins bending to the southwest and starts gradually ascending. Soon, though, the way is quite steep, and the trail will suck more calories than any Stairmaster. After about a mile of steep switchbacking, the grade relaxes. Soon, you'll cross a series of steep chutes that are often filled with snow into August, and sometimes year round. **Whoa!** Be careful of the snow bridges across these chutes, as they hide quick and rushing water.

Spring runoff crashes toward Weden Lake

Oof! After passing through a saddle, **4.5 miles**, the way levels into a basin of polished rock, the entrance to Gothic Basin. The official trail ends at several tarns, **4.7 miles**. A number of faint trails spur off to small campsites tucked across the basin. To the south, into the lower basin, you'll find Weden Lake and the plunging stream that feeds it wedged below Sheep Gap Mountain. To the north, you'll find Foggy Lake in the upper basin, sitting below Gothic and Del Campo Peaks. The views of Gothic and Del Campo, high, jagged, almost spiritual, are awesome.

Gazetteer

Nearby camping: Gold Basin Campground, Bedal Campground (primitive)
Nearest food, drink, services: Granite Falls

NOTES:

_____

_____

Hike 53 ⛰ ⛰ ⛰ ⛰
GLACIER BASIN–
MONTE CRISTO

Distance	**12.6-mile out and back**
Elevation	Low point: 2,360 ft., high point: 4,600 ft., **cumulative gain: 2,800 ft.**
Hike Time	5 to 8 hours, day hike or overnight
Travel	68 miles from Seattle
Season	Mid-July through mid-October
Maps	Green Trails: *Sloan Peak 111, Monte Cristo 143*
Restrictions	NW Forest Pass, dogs on leash, no fires, max group 12
More Info	Mt. Baker-Snoqualmie National Forest, Darrington District (Verlot), 360-691-7791, www.fs.fed.us/r6/mbs/

Trail Notes

The hike up to Glacier Basin is longer than the climb to Gothic Basin, but the trail isn't as rugged as its cousin basin to the west. To start, it's an easy hike up to the Monte Cristo townsite, and some just hike or bike there for the day. But from Monte Cristo the way is quite steep and occasionally rough. There's no lake or summit here, but the basin is impressively adorned by rocky peaks—Cadet, Monte Cristo, Kyes, and Columbia—small glaciers, and a flourish of wildflowers.

Driving Directions

From Everett, go east on US Highway 2, then east on State Highway 204, then north on State Hwy 9, and finally east on State Hwy 92 to Granite Falls, where State Hwy 92 becomes Stanley Street. Pass through Granite Falls, turn left on Mountain Loop Hwy toward Monte Cristo, and zero out your odometer. At 11 miles, pass the Verlot Ranger Station. At 30.8 miles, just before the road turns to dirt at Barlow Pass, turn left into the parking area for the trail to Monte Cristo.

Old railroad turntable at Monte Cristo

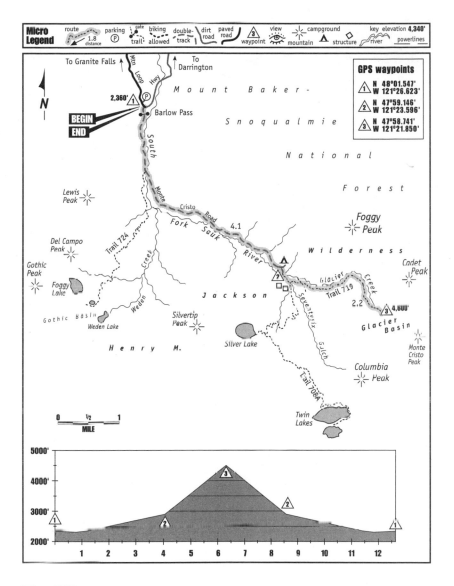

The Hike

To access the trail to Glacier Basin you have to hike up the dirt road, which begins across the Mountain Loop Hwy from the parking area, to the considerably-more-than-less abandoned mining town of Monte Cristo. Carefully cross the Mountain Loop Hwy, pass around a gate, and walk down the road to Monte Cristo, heading south. The way is flat and uninspired, save for some views of the

Foggy Peak and the rocky ridgeline above Glacier Basin

mountains, as it follows the South Fork of the Sauk River. At about **1.2 miles**, cross two former car bridges at Twin Bridge and continue south on the main road, now on the east side of the river.

At **3.8 miles**, stay to the right (Monte Cristo Campground is on the left). At **3.9 miles**, cross a footbridge over the river. A large metal sign proclaims the historical significance of the Monte Cristo Lodge, which no longer exists. From here, follow the wide trail toward Glacier Basin. A short distance farther, reach the actual Monte Cristo townsite. Be sure to check out the railroad turntable on the right. At the upper end of town, bear left to cross a bridge and walk up what used to be Dumas Street. At **4.2 miles**, after passing several former building sites, reach a four-way intersection: Go straight on Glacier Basin Trail 719.

Eastbound now, the trail climbs gently, first through the woods then through a brushy open area, all the while paralleling Glacier Creek. At around **5.2 miles**, the trail inclines steeply upward toward a rock face. After passing a waterfall on the left, the trail climbs, then cuts into a hanging valley. From here you can see the basin about one-quarter mile away. At **6.3 miles**, the main trail ends in the middle of Glacier Basin. You have arrived!

Gazetteer

Nearby camping: Gold Basin Campground, Bedal Campground (primitive)
Nearest food, drink, services: Granite Falls

NOTES:

_____

_____

Hike 54 ⛰️ ⛰️ ⛰️ ⛰️ ⛰️
TWIN LAKES

Distance	**17.2-mile out and back**
Elevation	Low point: 2,360 ft., high point: 5,500 ft., **cumulative gain: 4,900 ft.**
Hike Time	6 to 12 hours, day hike or overnight
Travel	68 miles from Seattle
Season	Mid-July through mid-October
Maps	Green Trails: *Sloan Peak 111*, *Monte Cristo 143*
Restrictions	NW Forest Pass, dogs on leash, no fires, max group 12
More Info	Mt. Baker-Snoqualmie National Forest, Darrington District (Verlot), 360-691-7791, www.fs.fed.us/r6/mbs/

Trail Notes

It used to be a bit of a death march to get to Twin Lakes. First the long road slog from the Mountain Loop Highway to Monte Cristo, followed by the foot climb up toward Silver Lake followed by a half bushwhack to Twin Lakes. Well, you'll still have to slog to Monte Cristo, but a completely new trail climbs up to Silver Lake, making this a much more enjoyable trip. It's an ambitious day hike, but good camp spots near Monte Cristo, Silver Lake, and beyond abound, all ready for the multi-day backpack.

Driving Directions

From Everett, go east on US Highway 2, then east on State Highway 204, then north on State Hwy 9, and finally east on State Hwy 92 to Granite Falls, where State Hwy 92 becomes Stanley Street. Pass through Granite Falls, turn left on Mountain Loop Hwy toward Monte Cristo, and zero out your odometer. At 11 miles, pass the Verlot Ranger Station. At 30.8 miles, just before the road turns to dirt at Barlow Pass, turn left into the parking area for the trail to Monte Cristo.

Monte Cristo townsite

The Hike

The route to Poodle Dog Pass—and what an excellent name for a high mountain pass!—and Twin Lakes beyond begins with a four-mile slog up the road to Monte Cristo, a more-than-less abandoned mining town. From the parking area, carefully cross the Mountain Loop Hwy, pass around a gate, and head down the road to Monte Cristo. The trail is mostly level and follows the South Fork of the Sauk River. At about **1.2 miles**, cross two bridges at Twin Bridge and continue

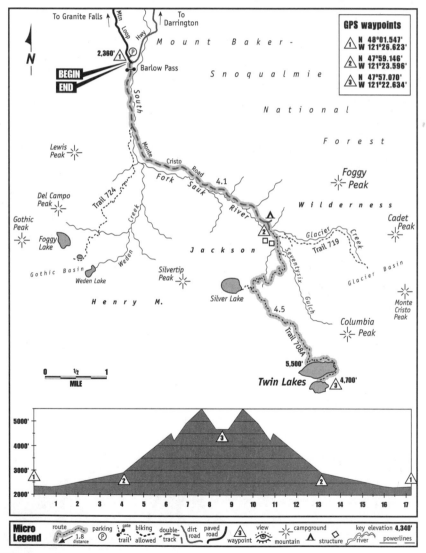

south on the main road, now on the east side of the river.

At **3.8 miles**, stay to the right (Monte Cristo Campground is on the left). At **3.9 miles**, cross a footbridge over the river. Ignore the old trail to Silver Lake on the right. A large metal sign proclaims the historical significance of the Monte Cristo Lodge, which now only exists in memory. From here, follow the wide trail. A short distance farther, reach the actual Monte Cristo townsite. At the far upper end of town, **4.1 miles**, cross the bridge on the right then pass between buildings to gain Trail 708 toward Poodle Dog Pass and Twin Lakes. After a steep pitch, pass by Sunday Falls and reach a fork—bear right.

Silver Lake

From here, the newly built trail ascends moderately. Around the **5.5-mile** mark, ignore the old trail on the right—bear left and continue the climbing, which is now steep. At **5.9 miles**, when the trail forks at the pass, bear left. (Silver Lake, in a cirque below Silvertip Peak, is a little more than one-quarter mile to the right.)

From the pass, the trail traverses the west slope of the ridge, climbing and dropping sharply, but mostly climbing to a high point above Twin Lakes. The views along the ridge get better and better, especially the cabal of peaks immediately east that surround Glacier Basin (see Hike 53). But the view from the rocky notch between Twin Peaks, east and west of the trail, which stand like a high, gated entrance to the pair of lakes below, is jaw-dropping. After passing through the notch between the peaks, the trail immediately breaks to the left and drops quickly to the two lakes. After rounding the east side of upper Twin Lake, the trail ends at the narrow knot of land between the lakes, **8.6 miles**.

Gazetteer
Nearby camping: Gold Basin Campground, Bedal Campground (primitive)
Nearest food, drink, services: Granite Falls

NOTES:

Hike 55 ⛰ ⛰ ⛰
GOAT LAKE

Distance	9.4-mile out and back
Elevation	Low point: 1,900 ft., high point: 3,200 ft., **cumulative gain: 1,700 ft.**
Hike Time	4 to 6 hours, day hike or overnight
Travel	73 miles from Seattle
Season	Mid-June through October
Map	Green Trails: *Sloan Peak 111*
Restrictions	NW Forest Pass, camping and fires prohibited within a quarter-mile of lake, dogs on leash, max group 12
More Info	Mt. Baker-Snoqualmie National Forest, Darrington District (Verlot), 360-691-7791, www.fs.fed.us/r6/mbs/

Trail Notes

With big evergreens and a sweet sort of meandering spirit, the first few miles up Lower Elliot Creek Trail would be a lovely stretch of trail even without the creek. But, with much help from my daughter and the rush and flow of the creek, I kept flashing on the Herkhiemer sisters, characters in Dr. Seuss' *The Sleep Book*. Each night before going to bed the sisters brush their teeth "Up at Herkhiemer Falls where the great river rushes and crashes down crags in great gargling gushes . . ." Well, the trail along Lower Elliot Creek reminds me of that line. Goat Lake has another sort of Dr. Seussian twist: Early in the twentieth century there was a hotel that supported the local mining community near the north end of the lake. It's gone now; it's hard to believe it ever existed. This trail is in good shape and moderately graded except for a few steep switchbacks just below the lake.

Driving Directions

From Everett, go east on US Highway 2, then east on State Highway 204, then north on State Hwy 9, and finally east on State Hwy 92 to Granite Falls, where State Hwy 92 becomes Stanley Street. Pass through Granite Falls, then turn left on Mountain Loop Highway toward Monte Cristo. Zero out your odometer here. At 11 miles, pass the Verlot Ranger Station. At 30.8 miles, the road turns to dirt as you cross Barlow Pass. At 34.3 miles, turn right on Forest Road 4080 toward Goat Lake Trail. At 35.3 miles, the road ends at the trailhead.

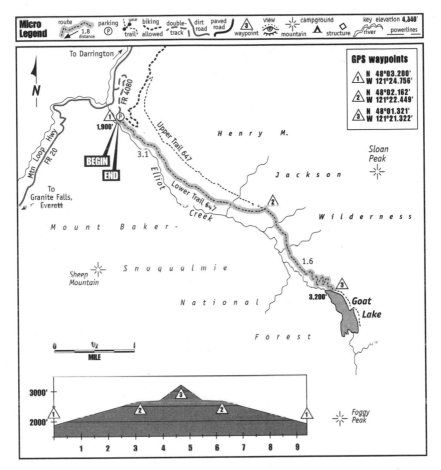

The Hike

Two trails start out from the Elliot Creek-Goat Lake Trailhead, and you can reach Goat Lake by following either. The old trail, Upper Elliot, bears left from the far end of the parking area and follows an old roadbed. This route is slightly easier, as the road gains elevation more slowly and the smooth, wide tread makes for easy walking, but it's also one-half mile farther and not as scenic. If you think seeing more country trumps beauty, then take Upper Elliot Trail on the way up. Otherwise, take Lower Elliot Trail both ways; it exits the parking lot on the right.

Immediately, Lower Elliot Trail drops steeply down toward Elliot Creek on a series of tight switchbacks. With the creek in view, you'll head southeast and begin ascending. The forest is dark for much of the way, heavy with fern-covered

177

Goat Lake

nurse logs, mossy rocks, and huge hemlocks and firs, though the creek opens a space in the tree cover and whitewater froth reflects the light on sunny days. The rich forest and gargling creek make magic the first few miles of the trail.

At **2.7 miles**, the trail eases away from the creek. By the time you rendezvous with Upper Elliot Trail, **3.1 miles**, you've only gained 700 feet. From the fork with the upper trail, bear right, walking through alders at first and then fir and hemlock again. For much of a mile the trail runs level, traversing the low, southwest slope of Sloan Peak. But around **3.8 miles**, the trail switchbacks up the narrow notch between Sloan Peak to the north and Foggy Peak to the south.

Elliot Creek has been a faint gargle for the past mile and a half, but as you climb, picking your way over rocks and roots and small streams of water, the roar of falls at the outlet of Goat Lake begins its crescendo. After a few more switchbacks, the crash of the water is loud, although unless you walk off-trail, you can't see the falls from below. You can, however, see the water vanish over the top of the falls, and you can also get a good look at the smaller but picturesque upper falls. Reach the north end of the lake at **4.7 miles**. A trail swings around the lake to the left, affording long views to the south end and the snowfields below Foggy and Cadet Peaks.

Gazetteer

Nearby camping: Beaver Creek Campground, Coal Creek Campground
Nearest food, drink, services: Granite Falls

NOTES:

_____

_____

178

Hike 56 ⛰️ ⛰️ ⛰️

BOULDER RIVER

Distance	8.6-mile out and back
Elevation	Low point: 960 ft., high point: 1,540 ft., **cumulative gain: 1,400 ft.**
Hike Time	3 to 4 hours, day hike
Travel	62 miles from Seattle
Season	March through November
Maps	Green Trails: *Oso 77, Granite Falls 109*
Restrictions	NW Forest Pass, dogs on leash, max group 12
More Info	Mt. Baker-Snoqualmie National Forest, Darrington District (Darrington), 360-436-1155, www.fs.fed.us/r6/mbs/

Trail Notes

Depending on the weather, you can hike this trail year round, and it's popular, in part, because of the long season. The waterfalls, big trees, and reasonable grade also make it a favorite. There's no destination here; it's a nectar-is-in-the-journey hike all the way.

One of many falls along Boulder River Trail

Driving Directions

Take Interstate 5 north of Everett to Exit 208. From there, take State Highway 530 east toward Darrington. About 24 miles east of I-5, immediately past milepost 41, turn right onto Forest Road 2010 and set your odometer to zero. **Whoa!** The turn onto FR 2010, which is narrow and starts out paved, is easily missed. At 3.9 miles, reach the trailhead on the right.

The Hike

Boulder River Trail 734 begins on an old logging railroad grade. The trail parallels Boulder River, below on the right, which rushes and tumbles its way toward the Stillaguamish River to the north. After about **0.5 mile**, as both the river and trail veer left, first heading south and then southeast, short furtive glimpses of Boulder Falls are visible through the trees downhill to the right.

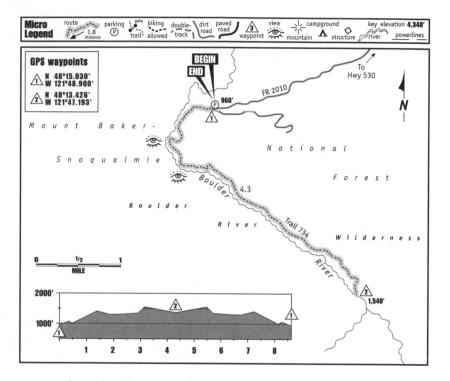

Just after a short but steep climb, ignore a spur trail on the right down to an old logging structure. Beyond the spur trail, enter the Boulder River Wilderness. At about **1.5 miles**, pass the route's most spectacular falls. A viewing bench offers a rest and viewpoint. From here, the trail runs along at the same level as the river.

After a while, the trail again climbs above the river, through a fir forest on a varying tread. Rocky and root-strewn in places, the trail meanders through the woods for a couple miles before descending back to the river. Reach the river at **4.3 miles**, the turnaround point. A faint, unmaintained trail continues across the river and up the broad northeast slope of Mount Ditney.

Gazetteer

Nearby camping: Squire Creek County Campground
Nearest food, drink, services: Darrington, Arlington

NOTES:

Hike 57 ⛰ ⛰ ⛰

PEEK-A-BOO LAKE

Distance	4.8-mile out and back
Elevation	Low point: 3,100 ft., high point: 4,380 ft., **cumulative gain: 2,350 ft.**
Hike Time	2 to 4 hours, day hike or overnight
Travel	83 miles from Seattle
Season	Mid-July through mid-October
Map	Green Trails: *Sloan Peak 111*
Restrictions	NW Forest Pass, dogs on leash
More Info	Mt. Baker-Snoqualmie National Forest, Darrington District (Darrington), 360-436-1155, www.fs.fed.us/r6/mbs/

Trail Notes

You know that liquor flask you stow away in your pack? If you're planning to camp at Peek-a-boo, you better fill it with DEET for this trip. This lake is out of the way, rugged and beautiful, and seems to have more than its fair share of mosquitoes. Some maps show an easy 600-foot gain, but there's a steep ridge to

Peek-a-boo Lake

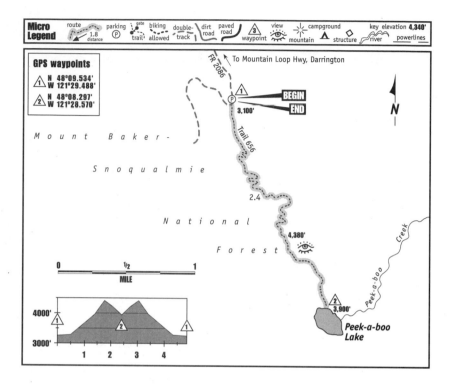

Micro Legend: route 1.8 distance · parking P · gate trail · biking allowed · double-track · dirt road · paved road · 3 waypoint · view · mountain · campground · structure · river · key elevation 4,340' · powerlines

GPS waypoints
△1 N 48°09.534'
   W 121°29.488'
△2 N 48°08.297'
   W 121°28.570'

FR 2086

To Mountain Loop Hwy, Darrington

N

1 P
BEGIN
END
3,100'

Trail 656

2.4

4,380'

Mount Baker -

S n o q u a l m i e

N a t i o n a l

F o r e s t

Creek

Peek-a-boo

2
3,900'

Peek-a-boo Lake

0   ½   1
MILE

4000' △1   △2   △1
3000'
     1   2   3   4

switchback up and over and then a descent down to the lake, which rests in a quiet, wooded pocket. With steep switchbacks and battalions of mosquitoes, why go? Peek-a-boo is a short hike and less travelled than most other Mountain Loop Highway hikes (in part because of the steep and narrow access road). There's a lovely meadow at the top of the ridge and the lake is peaceful, with several nice camp spots. Note, however, that the hike's north-facing aspect allows snow to linger late, and while the snow remains, it's not uncommon for hikers to lose the trail.

Driving Directions

Take Interstate 5 north of Everett to Exit 208, and proceed east on State Highway 530. After about 32 miles, reach Darrington, turn right onto the Mountain Loop Highway (Forest Road 20), and set your odometer to zero. At 9.2 miles, just before crossing the Sauk River, turn right on FR 2080. At 10.3 miles, turn right on FR 2081. Stay on the main road as you climb, ignoring two spurs on the left at 11.9 and 12.1 miles. At 13.7 miles, reach a fork and turn left on FR 2086. At 14.9 miles, reach a large berm that blocks the road. Park here.

The Hike

Cross over the berm and immediately bear left onto Trail 656 toward Peek-a-boo Lake. **Whoa!** Don't walk up the road. The trail traverses across a dark, north-facing slope, nearly level for the first half mile. The dark forest is an opportunity for Indian-pipe and coralroot, strange ghost-like stalks, to emerge from the forest duff and masquerade as wildflowers.

You'll begin the switchbacks soon enough, a few here, a short traverse, a few more, as you mount the sharp ridge. Then at **1.3 miles**, the trail heads up a steep draw, and the switchbacks seem to herringbone up the tight V toward the saddle. At **1.6 miles**, the way levels out and traverses across the top of several wet meadows. The sparse forest here affords views to the east toward Mount Pugh. Heading back into the forest again at **2.0 miles**, the trail passes between two modest hills and descends to the lake. In amongst the hemlock and fir, you'll see lots of weepy Alaska cedar. Reach the lakeshore at **2.4 miles**.

Gazetteer

Nearby camping: Clear Creek Campground (primitive)

Nearest food, drink, services: Darrington

NOTES:

_____

_____

_____

_____

Hike 58 ⛰ ⛰ ⛰
WHITE CHUCK BENCH

Distance	**13.4-mile out and back** (6.7-mile option)
Elevation	Low point: 1,060 ft., high point: 1,600 ft., **cumulative gain: 1,300 ft.**
Hike Time	5 to 7 hours, day hike
Travel	76 miles from Seattle
Season	May through mid-November
Map	Green Trails: *Sloan Peak 111*
Restrictions	NW Forest Pass, dogs on leash, no camping
More Info	Mt. Baker-Snoqualmie National Forest, Darrington District (Darrington), 360-436-1155, www.fs.fed.us/r6/mbs/

Trail Notes

The White Chuck River, tangled and wild, and fed by the White Chuck Glacier on the far south side of Glacier Peak, highlights this hike. The trail dips down to the river, climbs back into the woods, then drops back to the river again, over and over for the entire run of the route. Signed "WBT," White Chuck Bench Trail is really two trails: The first four miles intermittently follow an old roadbed through a young mixed forest. The trail is wide in places with long straight stretches—easy hiking. Over the final two and a half miles, the tread narrows to six inches in spots, the ups and downs get steeper, and the path is packed with roots. Elephantine strands of moss hang from the low branches of late-succession cedar, and ferns carpet the understory. All the while the White Chuck rushes on.

Driving Directions

Take Interstate 5 north of Everett to Exit 208, and proceed east on State Highway 530 . After about 32 miles, reach Darrington, turn right onto the Mountain Loop Highway (Forest Road 20), and set your odometer to zero. At 9.4 miles, cross over the Sauk River, then immediately turn left on FR 22. The road crosses the White Chuck River, then bends to the left. Ignore the river access road on the left. At 9.6 miles, the road divides: Turn right. Climb up this unmarked road, past a gravel pit, to White Chuck Bench Trailhead at 10.2 miles. Parking is on the left; the trail begins on the right.

White Chuck Bench Trail

The Hike

From the road, White Chuck Bench Trail 731 winds through the wet, mossy forest dominating the distinctive bench that separates the river from the wide slopes of White Chuck Mountain to the north. Over the first one and a half miles, the trail keeps the river at a distance. At **1.1 miles**, cross over a log bridge that spans Black Oak Creek. At **1.5 miles**, the trail angles toward the river, flirting with the river's bank for the rest of the route. At **3.6 miles**, cross a wide swath of rocks, which marks an old flood.

At **4.4 miles**, bear right onto a narrower trail. The wide corridor of the ancient roadbed ends here, and the wilder, narrower upper section of trail begins. From here, the trail winds and zigzags through a root garden, sometimes right along the river, sometimes on the slopes above it. Brilliant green ferns line stretches of the trail, in sharp contrast to olive-colored mosses that cling to rocks and soggy logs, hang from cedar branches, and climb red alder. At **6.5 miles**, reach a fork and bear right. The trail immediately drops into and climbs out of a short, but very steep, draw. From here, cross a series of single-log bridges that hop the numerous small streams which make up Crystal Creek. At **6.7 miles**, reach the trail's upper parking area along FR 23.

Option

You can always turn around to make this hike any distance you'd like. But if you have two vehicles, you can shuttle this hike, parking one car at the lower

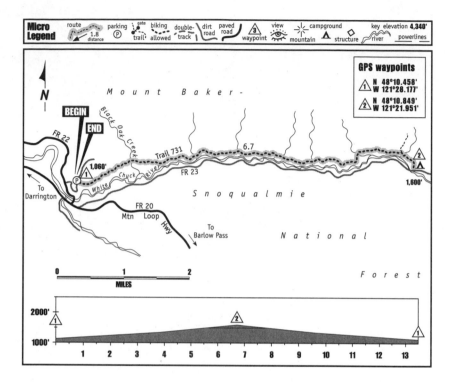

trailhead using the directions above, then beginning the hike from the upper trailhead. To reach the upper trailhead, set your odometer to zero, and drive back out to the Mountain Loop Highway (FR 20). Turn left, go less than one-quarter mile, and take the first left on FR 23. At 6.6 miles, immediately after crossing the river, park in the lot on the left side of the road, and follow the signs for the trail. This one-way trip is 6.7 miles.

Gazetteer

Nearby camping: Bedal Campground (primitive)

Nearest food, drink, services: Darrington

NOTES:

Hike 59 ⛰ ⛰ ⛰ ⛰ ⛰
MOUNT PUGH

Distance	11-mile out and back
Elevation	Low point: 1,900 ft., high point: 7,201 ft., **cumulative gain: 5,400 ft.**
Hike Time	6 to 10 hours, day hike
Travel	85 miles from Seattle
Season	Mid-July through mid-October
Map	Green Trails: *Sloan Peak 111*
Restrictions	NW Forest Pass, dogs on leash
More Info	Mt. Baker-Snoqualmie National Forest, Darrington District (Darrington), 360-436-1155, www.fs.fed.us/r6/mbs/

Trail Notes

As the crow flies, Glacier Peak's 10,541-foot summit stands just 12 miles east of Mount Pugh. But when you're standing among the granite rocks at the top of Pugh, staring out over the western arm of the Glacier Peak Wilderness, the volcano seems much closer. It's a magnificent view, well worth the 5,300-foot ascent. The big-tree forest and the spectacular late-season wildflowers below Stujack Pass vie for first runner-up, but the view of Glacier Peak is the highlight here. This is a tough day hike that doesn't really accommodate camping. As for the trail, it's as good as it gets for a route that climbs more than 1,000 feet a mile—smooth and walkable. Above the pass, though, the trail narrows and clings to the granite cracks along Pugh's western ridge. But beyond several airy sections and one short scramble, the trail remains good after the snow has melted.

Climbing toward Stujack Pass

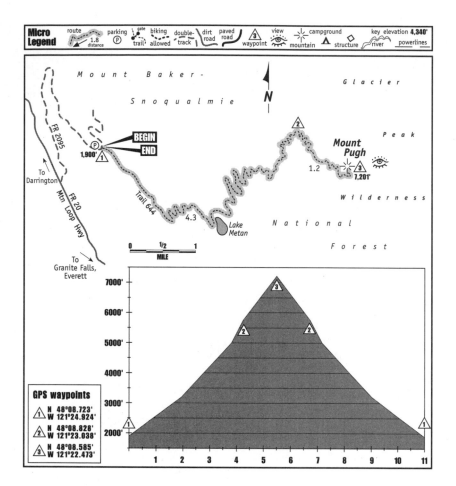

Micro Legend
route 1.8 distance parking (P) gate trail biking allowed double-track dirt road paved road 3 waypoint view mountain campground key elevation **4,340'** structure river powerlines

GPS waypoints
△1 N 48°08.723' W 121°24.924'
△2 N 48°08.828' W 121°23.038'
△3 N 48°08.585' W 121°22.473'

Mount Baker-Snoqualmie
Glacier Peak
Mount Pugh
7,201'
Wilderness National Forest
Lake Metan
Trail 644
FR 2095
FR 20 Mtn Loop Hwy
To Darrington
To Granite Falls, Everett
BEGIN END
1,900'
4.3
1.2

With snow on the trail, however, the knife-edge ridge above Stujack Pass is only one false step away from Madame Butterfly land, and it's best then to come back another time to bag the peak. A further note to would-be winter peak baggers: the trail has a wildlife closure from November 1 until just before Memorial Day.

Driving Directions

From Seattle, drive north on Interstate 5. Take Exit 208 and head east on State Highway 530 toward Darrington, about 32 miles east of I-5. In Darrington, turn right on Mountain Loop Highway (Forest Road 20), set your odometer to zero, and head southeast. At 9.5 miles, the road becomes dirt. At 13.2 miles, turn left on FR 2095, steep and rocky, toward the Mount Pugh Trailhead. At 14.8

On the sharp ridge above Stujack Pass

miles, park in the flat pulloff just before the switchback. The trail begins on the high side of the switchback.

The Hike

Mount Pugh Trail 644, narrow but smooth and well maintained, stakes a southeasterly traverse for the first mile. Through a mixed forest of red alder and hemlock, cedar and fir, the duff trail ascends at a steady rate, crossing two small creeks along the way. At **1.0 mile**, the trail begins switchbacking up the hillside, and the alder give way to a fully evergreen forest. Salal, Oregon grape, and moss cover the forest floor.

At **1.9 miles**, amid Alaska and red cedar, reach Lake Metan. There's a small campsite here, but the small, enclosed lake looks more mosquito breeding ground than pleasant midsummer camp spot. After winding around the north end of the lake, the trail again switchbacks up the steep forested western slopes of Mount Pugh. The ascent is more rigorous now.

At **3.8 miles**, pop out of the woods at the base of a formidable boulder and scree field. From here, it's a steep open climb up and across the rocky slope toward Stujack Pass, which is situated on the left side of the bowl. Despite the terrain and the incline, the trail is in remarkably good shape. Or perhaps you just don't notice the elevation gain as you wade through a rainbow of flowering paintbrush, thistle, mountain ash, columbine, and salmonberry. At **4.3 miles**, 800 feet above the base of the rocky slope, reach Stujack Pass, a dramatically whittled notch between high rock columns. It's best to turn around here if there's still any snow or if you're not a strong, agile hiker.

From the narrow pass, the trail ascends the ledges and cracks, through mountain hemlock and a few bushy white pines that cling to the mineral soil, and up the sharp ridgeline east toward the summit. At **4.8 miles**, pass by an old winch on a wood quad-pod used to haul supplies up to the mountaintop fire lookout that burned down years ago.

Whoa! Beyond the quad-pod, the trail continues climbing the knife-edge ridge, and several sections are exposed and airy. Around **5.1 miles**, there's a short scramble, but for the most part the trail negotiates the granite with well-placed tread. Above, the occasional cairn marks the trail, steep and sometimes faint, to the summit, **5.5 miles. Oof!**

Gazetteer

Nearby camping: Bedal Campground (primitive)
Nearest food, drink, services: Darrington

NOTES:

_____

_____

_____

_____

Hike 60 △

MUD MOUNTAIN RIM

Distance	4.2-mile out and back
Elevation	Low point: 1,250 ft., high point: 1,325 ft., **cumulative gain: 350 ft.**
Hike Time	1 to 2 hours, day hike
Travel	45 miles from Seattle
Season	Year round
Map	Green Trails: *Enumclaw 237*
Restrictions	Day use only
More Info	U.S. Army Corps of Engineers, 206-764-3717, www.nws.usace.army.mil/opdiv/mmd/index.htm

Trail Notes

On most nice days at Mud Mountain Dam Recreation Site—maintained by the U.S. Army Corps of Engineers—you'll find people standing at the lookout near the parking area staring down into the void of the White River Gorge. Nearby you'll find kids running across the grass, hurtling themselves toward swings and slides, jungle gyms and rope ladders. And the short, relatively easy hike along the rim, on a beautiful winding trail with views of the gorge, adds to the attraction. Note that mountain bikers also use this trail.

Driving Directions

From Seattle, head east on Interstate 90, south on I-405, then south on State Highway 169 to Enumclaw. In Enumclaw, take State Hwy 410 south toward Mount Rainier. As you leave town, pass milepost 26 and set your odometer to zero. At 3.9 miles, turn right on Mud Mountain Dam Road. At 6.4 miles, reach Mud Mountain Dam Recreation Site.

The Hike

From the parking area, head back to the entrance gate, then turn right and walk along the wide, gravel trail that parallels the fence. After about fifty yards, the trail elbows to the left away from the fence and begins following the canyon rim. At **0.3 mile**, the trail ends at a dirt road—bear right and walk along the road. At **0.5 mile**, take the trail on the left side of the

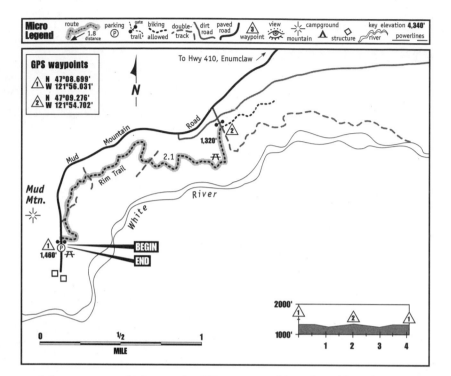

Micro Legend route 1.8 distance parking (P) gate biking trail allowed double-track dirt road paved road (3) waypoint view mountain campground structure key elevation 4,340' river powerlines

road that cuts around a large cedar. When you reach another old road at **0.8 mile**, turn right, then almost immediately turn left to regain the trail.

From here, the trail descends to a flat, boggy bench and noodles across a series of wood planks, past more cedar, skunk cabbage, and fern. At **1.2 miles**, the trail crosses another old dirt road, bears to the left, and passes an out-of-place outhouse. After a few more turns, you emerge from the darker forest and follow a wooden fence. The fence borders the cliffs that overlook the White River Gorge, **1.4 miles**. Just beyond this viewpoint, the trail bends away from the rim's edge and climbs for a short distance. At **2.1 miles**, reach a dirt road. Turn left to walk down to the river, or turn around to head back.

Gazetteer

Nearby camping: Kanaskat-Palmer State Park, The Dalles Campground
Nearest food, drink, services: Enumclaw

NOTES:

Hike 61 ⛰ ⛰

FEDERATION FOREST

Distance	6.6-mile out and back
Elevation	Low point: 1,585 ft., high point: 1,675 ft., **cumulative gain: 295 ft.**
Hike Time	2 to 4 hours, day hike
Travel	55 miles from Seattle
Season	Year round (main parking area closed November to March)
Map	Green Trails: *Greenwater 238*
Restrictions	State Parks vehicle fee, day use only, dogs on leash
More Info	Washington State Parks, 360-902-8844, www.parks.wa.gov

Trail Notes

Federation Forest State Park was donated to the state by the Washington State Federation of Women's Clubs. The federation wanted to save from the saw blade an area of easily accessible old growth, and they succeeded with this lovely forest filled with magnificent Douglas fir, hemlock, cedar, and spruce. The spots for sitting along the White River, the picnic area, and the great interpretive trails and center make this a perfect place for the family. The trail is a wonderful springtime hike, too, though it can be muddy. The downside: Though the rush of the river is charming, you can hear Highway 410 traffic noise from some sections of the trail.

Visiting the Hobbit House

Driving Directions

From Seattle, head east on Interstate 90, south on I-405, then south on State Highway 169 to Enumclaw. In Enumclaw, take State Hwy 410 south toward Mount Rainier. As you leave town, pass milepost 26 and set your odometer to zero. At 14 miles, pass the Federation Forest's west parking area on the right. At 15.9 miles, turn right at Federation Forest State Park, and park in the large paved parking area.

The Hike

From the parking area, walk to the right of the interpretive center to a kiosk. From the kiosk, follow the arrow to the West Trail Loop, ignoring four other trails that exit from this spot. At **0.2 mile**, reach a fork and bear right on the Nature Trail. At **0.6 mile**, when the trail joins the Old Naches Trail, bear right. Over the next few minutes, you'll pass two more forks in the trail—stay to the right each time.

At **0.9 mile**, you'll find another kiosk. Up to the right, there's a parking area and some restrooms along Hwy 410. Don't go up to the highway. Behind the kiosk, there are two trails—take the one on the right. With more roots jutting into its tread, the trail narrows, meandering past skunk cabbage and lady fern, gigantic Douglas fir, hemlock, spruce, and western red cedar, as planks, board-walks, and cut rounds help avoid the mucky spots. In several spots the trail tootles along the bank of the White River.

At **2.4 miles**, the trail widens again, revealing the spacing of an old road through a forest wet with fern, moss, and red alder. Along this stretch, known as Deadman Flat, ignore several lesser trails that spur off toward the river on the left. After a

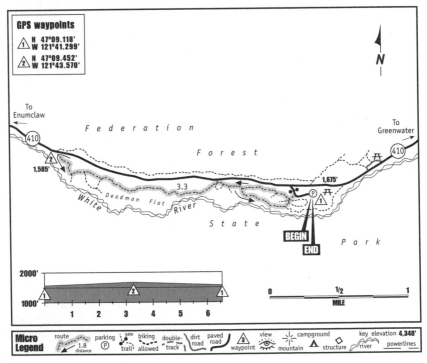

Dizzy from old growth

very gradual descent, the wide trail veers to the right and climbs easily up to a gate at Hwy 410, **3.3 miles**. From here, turn around and walk back to the interpretive center. When you reach the Old Naches Trail sign, you can vary the return trip by bearing to the right. From there, follow the signs back to the parking area.

Option

When you reach the far end, 3.3 miles, the trail crosses the highway and heads back toward the parking area on the north side of the highway. If loops mean a lot to you, take this route rather than walking the out and back described above. Be warned, though, that this north trail is wider, less maintained, and often runs within sight of the highway.

Gazetteer

Nearby camping: The Dalles Campground
Nearest food, drink, services: Greenwater

NOTES:

_____

_____

_____

_____

Hike 62 ⛰

GREENWATER LAKES

Distance	**4-mile out and back**
Elevation	Low point: 2,510 ft., high point: 3,150 ft., **cumulative gain: 800 ft.**
Hike Time	2 to 3 hours, day hike or overnight
Travel	68 miles from Seattle
Season	May through October
Map	Green Trails: *Lester 239*
Restrictions	NW Forest Pass
More Info	Mt. Baker-Snoqualmie National Forest, Snoqualmie District (Enumclaw), 360-825-6585, www.fs.fed.us/r6/mbs/

Trail Notes

These two small lakes offer a nice spot for a picnic and a good place to cast a line. But the highlight here is really the journey, past a tiny but interesting waterfall and along the Greenwater River, which rushes and pools through a miniature rock-formed gorge.

Driving Directions

From Seattle, head east on Interstate 90, south on I-405, then south on State Highway 169 to Enumclaw. In Enumclaw, take State Hwy 410 south toward Mount Rainier. As you leave town, pass milepost 26 and set your odometer to

zero. At 17 miles, pass through Greenwater. At 18.8 miles, turn left on Forest Road 70. At 28.5 miles, turn right on FR 7033 toward Greenwater River Trail. The road ends at the trailhead at 28.7 miles.

The Hike

From the large gravel parking area, head southeast on Trail 1176. The trail begins wide, graveled, and exposed, but soon ducks into a darker forest as it follows the Greenwater River. At **0.5 mile**, ignore a trail on the right. The firs and hemlocks are big here, and at **0.7 mile**, just after crossing the river, you'll pass an awe-inspiring western red cedar.

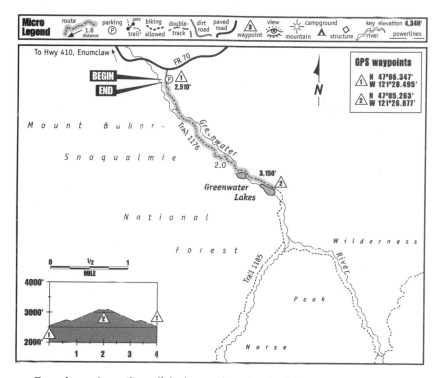

From here, the trail parallels the southern bank of the river and ascends gently. Around the **1.4-mile** mark, the river, swift and forceful yet calm, flows through a narrow rock gorge. It's a mesmerizing spot. At **1.6 miles**, a second bridge spans the gorge's rocky gap, providing a nice downstream view of the river. Almost immediately after the bridge, pass lower Greenwater Lake. Unless you are picnicking here, stay on the main trail, ignoring numerous desire paths and fishing trails on the right.

Continuing, the trail climbs a bit, crosses the river again, and arrives at upper Greenwater Lake at **2.0 miles**. You'll find a few camp spots just across the bridge at the far end of the lake.

Gazetteer

Nearby camping: The Dalles Campground
Nearest food, drink, services: Greenwater

NOTES:

Hike 63 ⛰ ⛰ ⛰
LOST LAKE

Distance	11-mile out and back (14.8-mile option)
Elevation	Low point: 2,510 ft., high point: 4,010 ft., **cumulative gain: 1,800 ft.**
Hike Time	4 to 7 hours, day hike or overnight
Travel	68 miles from Seattle
Season	July through October
Map	Green Trails: *Lester 239*
Restrictions	NW Forest Pass, max group 12
More Info	Mt. Baker-Snoqualmie National Forest, Snoqualmie District (Enumclaw), 360-825-6585, www.fs.fed.us/r6/mbs/

Trail Notes

Lost Lake sits in a forested pocket beneath Mutton Mountain and Dalles Ridge in the Norse Peak Wilderness. There are good campsites along the western shore of the lake; steep slopes advance to dramatic rocky crests on the east side. The hike up to the lake is pleasant, gradual and steady, through an old hemlock and fir forest. If you camp at the lake, you can leave your gear and hike up to Noble Knob and Dalles Ridge (see Hike 65).

Driving Directions

From Seattle, head east on Interstate 90, south on I-405, then south on State Highway 169 to Enumclaw. In Enumclaw, take State Hwy 410 south toward Mount Rainier. As you leave town, pass milepost 26 and set your odometer to zero. At 17 miles, pass through Greenwater. At 18.8 miles, turn left on Forest Road 70. At 28.5 miles, turn right on FR 7033 toward Greenwater River Trail. The road ends at the trailhead at 28.7 miles.

The Hike

From the large gravel parking area, hike southeast on Trail 1176. The trail begins wide and graveled as it follows the Greenwater River below on the right. At **0.5 mile**, ignore a trail on the right. The firs and hemlocks are big here, and at **0.7 mile**, just after crossing the river, you'll pass an awe-inspiring cedar.

The trail, a gradual ascent, continues to follow the river. Around the **1.4-mile** mark, the river rushes through a narrow rock gorge. At **1.6 miles**, a second bridge

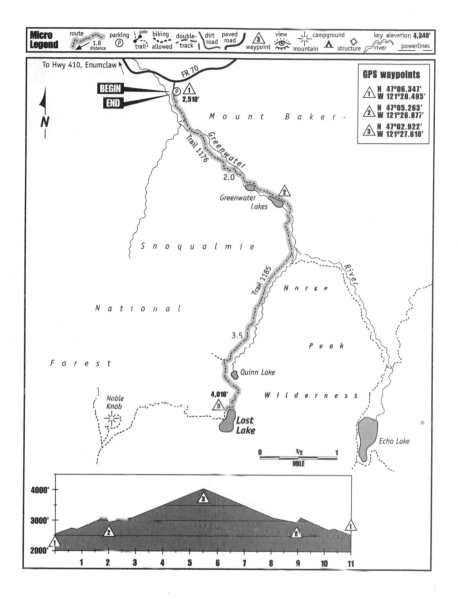

Micro Legend

route · 1.8 distance · parking ℗ · gate · biking trail · double-track · dirt road · paved road · ③ waypoint · view · mountain · campground · structure · river · key elevation **4,340'** · powerlines

To Hwy 410, Enumclaw

FR 70

BEGIN
END

℗ ①
2,510'

M o u n t   B a k e r -

Greenwater

Trail 1176

2.0

②

Greenwater
Lakes

S n o q u a l m i e

Trail 1185

N o r s e

River

N a t i o n a l

3.5

P e a k

F o r e s t

Quinn Lake

Noble
Knob

4,010' ③

W i l d e r n e s s

**Lost
Lake**

Echo Lake

0   ½   1
MILE

GPS waypoints

① N 47°06.347'
   W 121°28.495'

② N 47°05.263'
   W 121°26.877'

③ N 47°02.922'
   W 121°27.610'

4000'   ③
3000'   ②
2000'   ①

1 2 3 4 5 6 7 8 9 10 11

spans the gorge's rocky gap, providing an interesting downstream view of the river. Just after the bridge, pass lower Greenwater Lake. Stay on the main trail, ignoring numerous desire paths and fishing trails. Beyond the lower lake, the trail crosses the river, climbs a bit, crosses the river again, and arrives at upper Greenwater Lake, **2.0 miles**. There are a few camp spots at the far end of the lake.

199

Greenwater River

Above upper Greenwater Lake, the trail climbs through a darker forest, descends briefly, enters the Norse Peak Wilderness, then climbs again to a fork at **3.1 miles**. Bear right, following the sign to Lost Lake. It's here that the trail leaves the melodies of the Greenwater River, and follows a small tributary that originates from Quinn Lake. At **4.5 miles**, ignore a lesser, unmarked trail on the right. After a short but steady climb, you'll emerge from woods and pass through a small, rocky meadow. Noble fir, Alaska cedar, meadow wildflowers, and crisp air trumpet the subalpine zone. At **5.5 miles**, reach Lost Lake.

Option

If you take the left fork at 3.1 miles, you'll continue to follow the Greenwater River toward Echo Lake. Bear right at the fork at 5.6 miles, and reach Echo Lake at 7.4 miles, making it a 14.8-mile day hike.

Gazetteer

Nearby camping: The Dalles Campground
Nearest food, drink, services: Greenwater

NOTES:

_____

_____

_____

_____

Hike 64 ⛰ ⛰ ⛰
SNOQUERA FALLS

Distance	4.6-mile loop
Elevation	Low point: 2,450 ft., high point: 3,180 ft., **cumulative gain: 850 ft.**
Hike Time	2 to 3 hours, day hike
Travel	66 miles from Seattle
Season	June through mid-October
Map	Green Trails: *Greenwater 238*
Restrictions	NW Forest Pass
More Info	Mt. Baker-Snoqualmie National Forest, Snoqualmie District (Enumclaw), 360-825-6585, www.fs.fed.us/r6/mbs/

Trail Notes
The Snoquera Falls loop is short, and the cumulative elevation gain is modest. But crossing the creek at the top near the falls is tricky, and the rocky descent is somewhat herky-jerky. For an easier route, follow the hike directions up to the falls then turn around to make this an out-and-back trip. The falls are impressive, especially when the late spring runoff is in full flow.

Driving Directions
From Seattle, head east on Interstate 90, south on I-405, then south on State Highway 169 to Enumclaw. In Enumclaw, take State Hwy 410 south toward Mount Rainier. As you leave town, pass milepost 26 and set your odometer to zero. At 26.8 miles (just before milepost 53), turn left on Forest Road 7155. At 26.9 miles, turn right into the Camp Sheppard Trailhead parking area.

The Hike
The unmarked trail starts out from the back of the paved parking area. After crossing an old roadbed, reach a fork at **0.1 mile** and bear left. At **0.2 mile**, reach another fork and go left again. The trail soon widens considerably and climbs to a T at **0.3 mile**. Turn right at the T, and then almost immediately reach a fork and bear left on Snoquera Falls Loop Trail 1167. From here, climb through an open hemlock and Douglas fir forest.

At **0.6 mile**, reach a T and turn left. After a mile of switchbacks and traversing ascents, reach Snoquera Falls, **1.6 miles**. From the view below the falls, the pali-

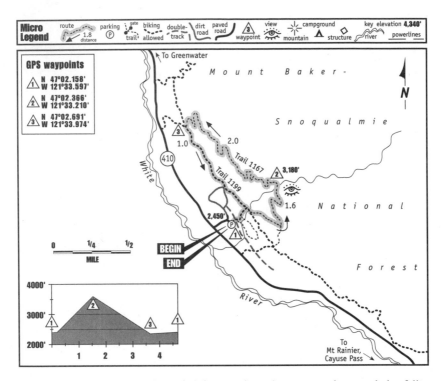

sades shoot up almost a thousand feet, and rainbows in and around the falling water are common. The trail continues across the creek—it's a steep, rocky descent, and sometimes the trail is difficult to follow.

At **3.6 miles**, reach a four-way intersection—turn left on White River Trail 1199. When you reach an unmarked fork at **3.9 miles**, bear left. Just beyond this fork, the trail crosses a field at Camp Sheppard. At **4.1 miles**, follow the trail sign, which points toward Snoquera Falls Junction. **Whoa!** The route past Camp Sheppard is somewhat confusing—stay to the left and keep the roads and buildings of the camp on your right. At **4.3 miles**, reach another four-way, turn right, and follow the signs toward the trailhead. Arrive there at **4.6 miles**.

Gazetteer

Nearby camping: The Dalles Campground, Silver Springs Campground
Nearest food, drink, services: Greenwater

NOTES:

_____

_____

Hike 65 ⛰ ⛰ ⛰
NOBLE KNOB

Distance	7.4-mile out and back
Elevation	Low point: 5,600 ft., high point: 6,050 ft., **cumulative gain: 1,900 ft.**
Hike Time	4 to 5 hours, day hike or overnight
Travel	75 miles from Seattle
Season	Mid-July through mid-October
Map	Green Trails: *Lester 239*
Restrictions	NW Forest Pass, max group 12
More Info	Mt. Baker-Snoqualmie National Forest, Snoqualmie District (Enumclaw), 360-825-6585, www.fs.fed.us/r6/mbs/

Trail Notes

Easy hiking most of the way, this ridgeline trail sneaks in climbs of 200 feet here, 400 feet there, and it adds up by the end of the day. The views into adjacent Norse Peak Wilderness and across the White River valley to Mount Rainier are terrific. Note that the views of Rainier are much better if you hike this trail in the morning, when the sun projects light onto the mountain's slopes at an angle from the east rather than from directly above the mountain. Across the open ridge, the wildflowers bloom bright in July and August. The exposed meadows can be hot— another good reason to start out early. Camping sites are available just below Noble Knob at George Lake or to the east at Lost Lake.

Driving Directions

From Seattle, head east on Interstate 90, south on I-405, then south on State Highway 169 to Enumclaw. In Enumclaw, take State Hwy 410 south toward Mount Rainier. As you leave town, pass milepost 26 and set your odometer to zero. At 30 miles (milepost 56), turn left on Forest Road 7174, a.k.a. Corral Pass

Noble Knob

Road. What follows is a very steep dirt road. At 30.5 miles, stay to the left, following the signs to Corral Pass. At 36 miles, reach a T and turn left. The road ends at the trailhead, 36.2 miles.

The Hike

Take Noble Knob Trail 1184. The narrow trail traverses an open hillside, which can be quite hot. Reach a T at **0.5 mile**, and turn left. The trail is wide for a short distance, following an old road, then narrows and continues to traverse north, riding the contours of the ridge's west flank. The sparsely forested ridge affords excellent views of Mount Rainier to the west and Norse Peak Wilderness to the east. Stay on the main trail, ignoring a few faint spurs. Reach a fork at **1.4 miles**, and bear left.

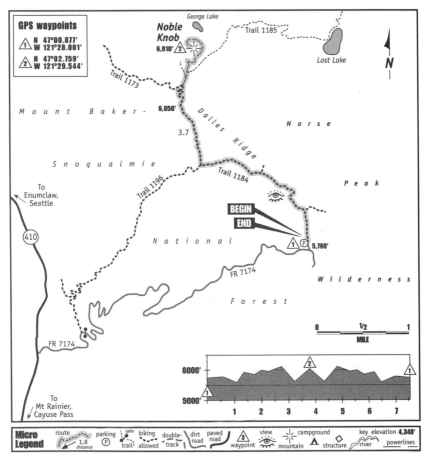

Dalles Ridge

From here, the trail descends then climbs over a notch in the ridgeline, then traverses again, now in heavier forest. Reach an intersection at **1.9 miles** and bear right, remaining on Noble Knob Trail 1184 toward 28 Mile Road. Continue north across the high, western side of Dalles Ridge—this is a beautiful section of trail, with noble and silver fir shading the way.

At **2.8 miles**, the trail crosses to the east side of the ridge and switchbacks steeply down a brushy, open slope. Noble Knob, cone-shaped and almost bare of trees, is directly north. Reach a T at **3.1 miles** and turn right. At **3.3 miles**, reach a fork and bear right. A few strides farther, reach another fork and bear left. From here, the trail cuts to the left then switchbacks to the right to mount Noble Knob counterclockwise. At the top, **3.7 miles**, check out the views of George Lake below and Lost Lake farther down to the east.

Gazetteer

Nearby camping: Silver Springs Campground

Nearest food, drink, services: Greenwater

NOTES:

_____

_____

_____

_____

Hike 66 ⛰ ⛰ ⛰
CRYSTAL LAKES

Distance	**6-mile out and back**
Elevation	Low point: 3,500 ft., high point: 5,830 ft., **cumulative gain: 2,400 ft.**
Hike Time	3 to 5 hours, day hike or overnight
Travel	75 miles from Seattle
Season	Mid-July to early-October
Map	Green Trails: *Mount Rainier East 270*
Restrictions	No dogs, no fires, permit required for camping
More Info	Mount Rainier National Park, 360-569-2211, www.nps.gov/mora/

Trail Notes

Climbing 800 feet per mile is beyond the comfort level for some, but that's the drill if you want to hike to Crystal Lakes. It's not a difficult trail—it's smooth and well maintained—it's just steep. The lower part of the ascent offers views through the trees of Mount Rainier, but the highlights of the trip are the bright July wildflowers that blanket the meadows and the jagged peaks that surround the lakes basin. Despite the ascent, this is a popular hike, in part because it doesn't require the national park entrance fee.

Driving Directions

From Seattle, head east on Interstate 90, south on I-405, then south on State Highway 169 to Enumclaw. In Enumclaw, take State Hwy 410 south toward Mount Rainier. As you leave town, pass milepost 26 and set your odometer to zero. At 35.7 miles (before reaching milepost 62), find a small, easily missed trailhead along Hwy 410 on the left. This is Crystal Lakes Trailhead.

Columbine

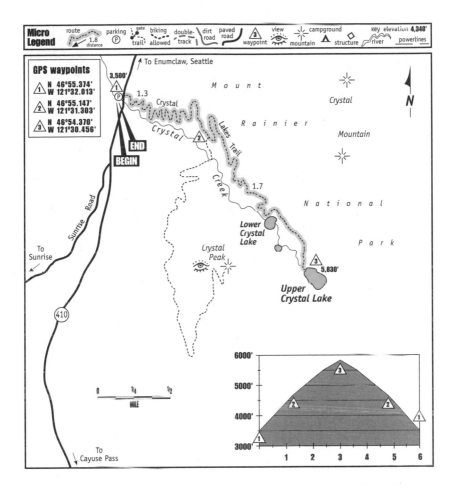

The Hike

The first few hundred yards of the Crystal Lakes Trail ascend manageably through fir and hemlock. But then the switchbacking begins and doesn't really stop until you've reached lower Crystal Lake. The trail grinds doggedly up the massive western slope of Crystal Mountain. At the turns from several switchbacks, there's a queasy view down the ravine that guides Crystal Creek.

At **1.3 miles**, reach a fork and bear left toward Crystal Lakes. (The right fork toward Crystal Peak affords spectacular views of Mount Rainier, many fewer people, and a peak to bag, but there's little shade on the trail and no lake at the end.) After another switchback or two, the trail gives up on the dramatic zigzags. It twists and

Crystal Lake

bends but mostly traverses up the small, sparsely forested valley, keeping the creek below on the right.

At **2.3 miles**, reach another fork at the north end of Lower Crystal Lake: Bear left and walk toward Upper Crystal Lake. (The right fork leads to a campsite.) From here, the subalpine firs are spread thin, and the route blazes with wildflowers in late July and August. At **3.0 miles**, reach the upper lake. A craggy and formidable rock bowl, rising 1,000 feet above, cups the south end of the lake, and elk and mountain goats aren't uncommon sights in the small tufts of green that pepper the crags. You can return the way you came, but on a clear day a side trip out the Crystal Peak Trail will present an open-face view of Rainier.

Gazetteer

Nearby camping: Silver Springs Campground
Nearest food, drink, services: Greenwater

NOTES:

_____

_____

_____

_____

Hike 67 ⛰ ⛰ ⛰

SUMMER LAND

Distance	**8.4-mile out and back**
Elevation	Low point: 3,800 ft., high point: 5,960 ft., **cumulative gain: 2,200 ft.**
Hike Time	3 to 6 hours, day hike or overnight
Travel	79 miles from Seattle
Season	Mid-July through September
Map	Green Trails: *Mount Rainier East 270*
Restrictions	Mount Rainier National Park entrance fee, no dogs, no fires, permit required for camping
More Info	Mount Rainier National Park, 360-569-2211, www.nps.gov/mora/

Trail Notes

My brother describes the hike to Summer Land as the "Mount Si of Mount Rainier National Park." On summer weekends the trail is truly that crowded—it's the amazing wildflowers and awesome views of Rainier that draw the people in. It's less crowded, though, if you can time it just right: a crisp, blue day in late September before the park service closes the gate. And it's then you can see why it's so popular—this smooth, wide duff trail winding through old growth cedar and fir. You'll still get the awe-inspiring views of the mountain in the fall, but the

Mount Rainier from Summerland Trail

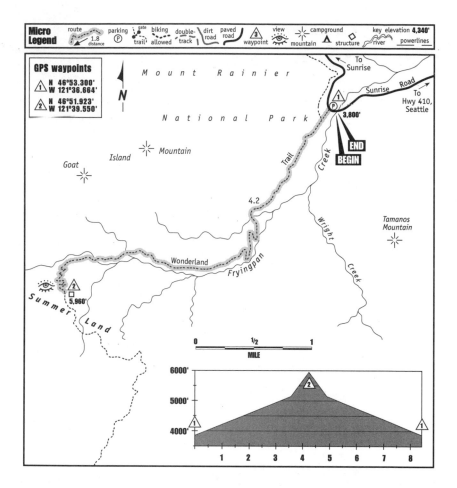

wildflowers are usually gone and it can snow anytime. Note: The meadows at the top are very fragile, so always stay on the trail.

Driving Directions

From Seattle, head east on Interstate 90, south on I-405, then south on State Highway 169 to Enumclaw. In Enumclaw, take State Hwy 410 south toward Mount Rainier. As you leave town, pass milepost 26 and set your odometer to zero. Just past milepost 62, 36.2 miles from Enumclaw, turn right on Sunrise Road, following the sign to Sunrise. Pass through the national park fee booth at 37.6 miles. At 40.5 miles, pull off into the small parking area on the right, just beyond the bridge over Fryingpan Creek. Note: Ten cars max out the small parking area at the trailhead and, though it's common, the Park Service discourages people from parking alongside the road.

The Hike

The trail begins across the road from the parking area. After a few hundred yards, reach a fork at the Wonderland Trail and bear left. From here, the wide duff trail pushes south, paralleling Fryingpan Creek at a distance. It's a mixed forest, with Douglas, silver, and noble firs and Alaska and red cedar, and many of the trees are enor-

Advice to live by

mous. For the first mile, the trail gains elevation slowly. It's quiet—if you're smart or lucky enough to have avoided the crowds—and somewhat dark.

At about **1.5 miles**, the trail traverses to an overlook into the shallow Fryingpan Creek canyon. From here, the trail gains elevation more quickly and follows the rush of the creek more closely. But the trail is still wide and smooth and the walking easy. At **2.8 miles**, emerge from the trees and follow the trail west up the narrow valley. Ahead to the west, bits and pieces of Mount Rainier become visible, but the mountain feels almost too close, and you can't see it or take it all in at once. The Emmons Glacier appears, and then Little Tahoma Peak and parts of the Fryingpan Glacier, headwaters of the creek.

At **3.6 miles**, the trail bends south again and begins a steep set of switchbacks that climb toward the saddle at Summer Land. The trail is in good condition and the switchbacks are thoughtfully graded, however this steep hillside is the most difficult part of the trail. At **4.0 miles**, reach a high sloping meadow that offers up excellent views of the mountain. At **4.2 miles**, reach the sleeping shelter at Summer Land. It's a perfect place for lunch, and the trail beyond, toward Panhandle Gap and Indian Bar, beckons enticingly.

Gazetteer

Nearby camping: White River Campground
Nearest food, drink, services: Greenwater

NOTES:

_____

_____

Hike 68 ▲▲▲

GLACIER BASIN–
MOUNT RAINIER

Distance	6-mile out and back
Elevation	Low point: 4,280 ft., high point: 5,960 ft., **cumulative gain: 1,800 ft.**
Hike Time	2 to 4 hours, day hike or overnight
Travel	82 miles from Seattle
Season	Mid-July through September
Map	Green Trails: *Mount Rainier East 270*
Restrictions	Mount Rainier National Park entrance fee, no dogs, no fires, permit required for camping
More Info	Mount Rainier National Park, 360-569-2211, www.nps.gov/mora/

Trail Notes

This is a climber's trail: Businesslike it shoots straight up the valley without wasting too much time or energy. Though the majority of climbers take the Camp Muir route on the south side of Rainier to approach the summit, some begin their ascent on this trail. Leaving the White River Campground, they ascend the mountain from the east, first on the Inter Glacier and then up an ever-changing route between the Emmons and Winthrop Glaciers. Climber's business notwithstanding, it's a beautiful trail along the Inter Fork of the White River. The trail is at first lightly forested and then moves into the open past the ragged tailings at the dirty

Glacier Basin and Mount Rainier from Burroughs Mountain

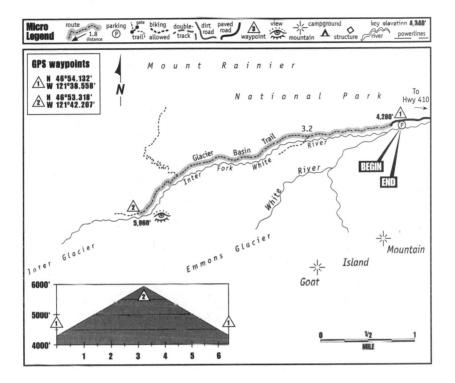

Micro Legend: route · 1.8 distance · parking (P) · gate trail · biking allowed · double-track · dirt road · paved road · (9) waypoint · view mountain · campground · structure · key elevation 4,340' · river · powerlines

GPS waypoints
1 N 46°54.132' W 121°38.558'
2 N 46°53.318' W 121°42.207'

end of the Emmons Glacier. Steep when it has to be but generally moderately graded, the path features eye-popping views of the mountain along the way. Also of note: The hike to Glacier Basin is shorter and less of a climb than is the trail to Summer Land (see Hike 67).

Driving Directions

From Seattle, head east on Interstate 90, south on I-405, then south on State Highway 169 to Enumclaw. In Enumclaw, take State Hwy 410 south toward Mount Rainier. As you leave town, pass milepost 26 and set your odometer to zero. Just past milepost 62, 36.2 miles from Enumclaw, turn right on Sunrise Road, following the sign to Sunrise. Pass through the national park fee booth at 37.6 miles. At 41.5 miles, turn left toward White River Campground. Pass through the campground, 43 miles, and park in the hiker/climber parking area near the trailhead.

The Hike

Walk a short distance to the west end of the campground to find the start of the Glacier Basin Trail. Parts of the trail follow the route of an old mining road,

213

Alpine asters grow out of the pumice

paralleling the Inter Fork on the north. The first section climbs at a modest rate, traversing the open forest that affords almost continuous views down to the river and intermittent views of Mount Rainier. The valley is wedged between Goat Island Mountain to the south and Burroughs Mountain to the north, both broad and tall. At **0.9 mile**, reach a fork and bear right. (The left fork heads out a mile for a better view of the huge moraine at the bottom of the Emmons Glacier.)

From the fork, the way opens up even more, and the hiking can be hot on sunny days. The trail crosses several small creeks that crash 2,000 feet down the south slopes of Burroughs Mountain. You'll hit several steep sections in the trail. At **2.4 miles**, reach a fork and bear left, following the river and heading straight for the mountain. Can't miss it. At **3.0 miles**, the valley opens up into Glacier Basin, and you'll reach the wilderness camps there. This is the turnaround point, though the climber's trail continues up to the Inter Glacier and Camp Schurman above.

Gazetteer

Nearby camping: White River Campground
Nearest food, drink, services: Greenwater

NOTES:

_____

_____

_____

_____

Hike 69 ⛰ ⛰ ⛰
UPPER PALISADES LAKE

Distance	6.8-mile out and back
Elevation	Low point: 5,520 ft., high point: 6,080 ft., **cumulative gain: 2,100 ft.**
Hike Time	3 to 5 hours, day hike or overnight
Travel	88 miles from Seattle
Season	Mid-July through September
Map	Green Trails: *Mount Rainier East 270*
Restrictions	Mount Rainier National Park entrance fee, no dogs, no fires, permit required for camping
More Info	Mount Rainier National Park, 360-569-2211, www.nps.gov/mora/

Trail Notes

This is one of the few hikes, in this book at least, that originates at the high point and drops into the lake. It's a nice way to go, except when you're ready to return from the lake and you're facing a climb back to the trailhead. This is also one of those rare Mount Rainier hikes—you paid that entrance fee, forgodsakes—that doesn't afford those outstanding views of cracked glaciers and the 14,410-foot summit. Head somewhere else for the views. Here you'll pass six mountain lakes as the trail rolls, climbing and descending, past wildflowered meadows and sheer rock cliffs. The trail is usually smooth and in great shape.

Driving Directions

From Seattle, head east on Interstate 90, south on I-405, then south on State Highway 169 to Enumclaw. In Enumclaw, take State Hwy 410 south toward Mount Rainier. As you leave town, pass milepost 26 and set your odometer to zero. Just past milepost 62, 36.2 miles from Enumclaw, turn right, following the sign to Sunrise. Pass through the national park fee booth at 37.6 miles. At 49.1 miles, park at the Sunrise Point parking area.

Palisades Lake

215

The Hike

From the paved pullout of Sunrise Point along heavily touristed Sunrise Road, the Palisades Trail descends along the top of Sunrise Ridge. At **0.3 mile**, the wide, sometimes dusty trail switchbacks to the left, leaving the ridgetop and dropping quickly. After crossing a talus slope, home of many a whistling marmot, reach a fork, **0.5 mile**, and bear right, continuing toward Upper Palisades Lake.

The trail is level and smooth, and it meanders across the small basin bookended by Sunrise and Clover Lakes. The basin is a patchwork of postage-stamp meadows and small groves of noble fir and mountain hemlock. At **1.4 miles**, reach Clover Lake. From here, the trail climbs a forested ridge to a saddle that sits between a solitary prow to the east and the high ridge of the Sourdough Mountains to the west. Descend from the saddle into another lakes basin and head north.

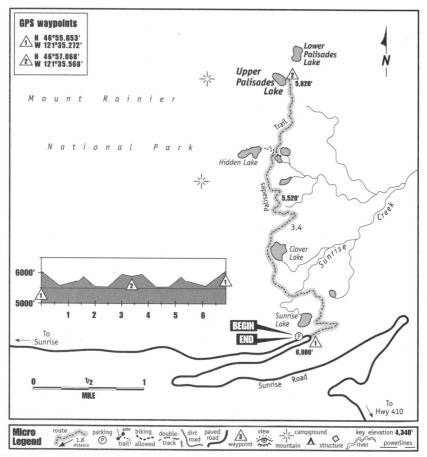

GPS waypoints

1. N 46°55.053' W 121°35.272'
2. N 46°57.068' W 121°35.568'

Lower Palisades Lake

N

Upper Palisades Lake · 2 · 5,820'

Mount Rainier

National Park

Trail

Hidden Lake

Palisades · 5,520'

Creek

3.4

Clover Lake

Sunrise

6000'

2 · 1

5000' · 1

1 2 3 4 5 6

To Sunrise

Sunrise Lake

BEGIN
END · P · 1

6,080'

0 ½ 1

MILE

Sunrise Road

To Hwy 410

Micro Legend — route · 1.8 distance · parking ⓟ · gate · biking trail allowed · double-track · dirt road · paved road · 3 waypoint · view 👁 · mountain · campground · structure · key elevation 4,340' · river · powerlines

216

On the way toward Palisades Lake

At **2.6 miles**, reach Tom, Dick, and Harry Lakes. Bear to the right at the fork, continuing toward Palisades Lake. (The left fork climbs steeply to picturesque Hidden Lake.) From here, the trail climbs gently, and the way soon opens up into a large meadow, bursting with wildflowers and insects in July and August. You'll find Upper Palisades Lake, tucked beneath the angular palisades, just beyond and below the meadow, **3.4 miles**.

Gazetteer

Nearby camping: White River Campground

Nearest food, drink, services: Greenwater

NOTES:

_____

_____

_____

_____

Hike 70 ▲ ▲
GREEN LAKE

Distance	3.6-mile out and back
Elevation	Low point: 2,100 ft., high point. 3,200 ft., **cumulative gain: 1,200 ft.**
Hike Time	1 to 3 hours, day hike
Travel	66 miles from Seattle
Season	Mid-June through mid-October
Map	Green Trails: *Mount Rainier West 269*
Restrictions	Mount Rainier National Park entrance fee, no dogs, no camping, no fires
More Info	Mount Rainier National Park, 360-569-2211, www.nps.gov/mora/

Trail Notes

Here's a short, relatively easy hike to a small mountain lake. Parts of the route are steep, but the trail is mostly smooth and well maintained. It's a delightful hike, and the magic here comes in the form of bright green fern corridors, towering old growth, and dancing Ranger Creek Falls. After such a beautiful trail, don't be surprised if the lake seems a bit disappointing.

Driving Directions

From Seattle, head east on Interstate 90, south on I-405, then south on State Highway 169 to Enumclaw. At the junction of Hwy 169 and Hwy 410 in Enumclaw, set your odometer to zero and take Hwy 410 west to Buckley. At 6 miles, turn left on Hwy 165 toward Carbonado. At 16.8 miles, reach a fork and go left, toward the Carbon River. At 25 miles, pass the Carbon River Ranger Station. At 28.2 miles, park in the small parking area on the left.

The Hike

From the small parking area, cross the road to the trailhead. The trail, smooth, wide, and well used, wanders through old growth and fern gardens, lush and moss-strewn. After a few meanders, the trail begins

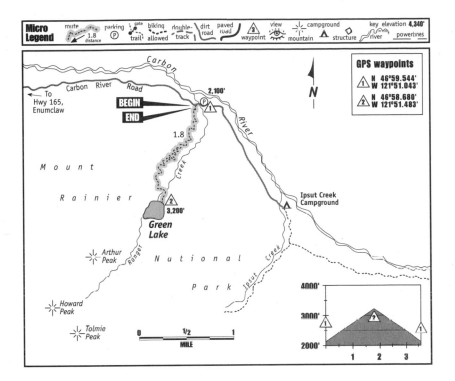

climbing the sharp valley between Arthur and Gove Peaks. Ferns line the trail and, mixed with moss and saplings that feed from enormous nurse logs, create a green kaleidoscope of patterns and images. The nurse logs, though, aren't the only enormous things here. Huge cedar and Douglas fir tower over the trail and loom out over Ranger Creek.

The trail, climbing continuously, alternates between smooth duff and rocky stairsteps. At **1.0 mile**, reach a fork and bear right. (The left fork spurs down to a spectacular and recommended view of Ranger Falls a short distance away.) At **1.4 miles**, the ascent eases and crosses Ranger Creek. After a short descent, reach Green Lake at **1.8 miles**.

Gazetteer

Nearby camping: Ipsut Creek Campground

Nearest food, drink, services: Carbonado

NOTES: